Microsoft Hyper-V PowerShell Automation

Manage, automate, and streamline your Hyper-V environment effectively with advanced PowerShell cmdlets

Vinith Menon

BIRMINGHAM - MUMBAI

Microsoft Hyper-V PowerShell Automation

First published: January 2015

Production reference: 1230115

Published by Packt Publishing Ltd.
Livery Place
35 Livery Street
Birmingham B3 2PB, UK.

ISBN 978-1-78439-153-9

www.packtpub.com

Credits

Author

Vinith Menon

Reviewers

Alexander Kellett

Roy Verrips

Commissioning Editor

Dipika Gaonkar

Acquisition Editor

Sonali Vernekar

Content Development Editor

Priyanka Shah

Technical Editors

Pragnesh Bilimoria

Edwin Moses

Copy Editors

Gladson Monteiro

Jasmine Nadar

Project Coordinator

Neha Thakur

Proofreaders

Simran Bhogal

Maria Gould

Ameesha Green

Paul Hindle

Indexer

Monica Ajmera Mehta

Production Coordinator

Conidon Miranda

Cover Work

Conidon Miranda

About the Author

Vinith Menon has extensive experience in the IT industry. At the beginning of his career, he was working with a leading consulting firm as a senior systems engineer managing Windows Server and the VMware virtualization environment. He was also extensively involved in automation using scripting.

Later, he worked with another platinum-level consulting company as a senior software engineer and managed Microsoft Hyper-V and NetApp environments for Avanade using PowerShell scripting. Vinith has done automation for tasks that earlier required manual work using Opalis and integrated them with PowerShell scripting. He has also built integration packs using PowerShell for Microsoft System Center Orchestrator. He has extensive knowledge of Hyper-V and the management of virtual machine environments using System Center Virtual Machine Manager. He has in-depth technical expertise in PowerShell scripting, Active Directory, server administration, and network management.

Vinith is now part of Microsoft Business Unit Technology Evangelism with NetApp. At the moment, he is interested in the automation of various PowerShell scripting, Microsoft Hyper-V virtualization, Microsoft Exchange, and System Center technologies such as SCSM, SCOM, and SCORCH 2012. As a subject matter expert of Hyper-V and PowerShell, he blogs and supports the NetApp PowerShell community.

Vinith is very passionate about automation and PowerShell scripting. You can find him frequently blogging about virtualization, PowerShell, and all automation-related information that deals with Microsoft System Center, Windows Server, and client operating systems. He is also an active member of the PowerShell Bangalore User Group and loves sharing his knowledge with like-minded techies.

About the Reviewers

Alexander Kellett is a relatively recent convert to the Windows world after many years of Linux and Mac OS X experience. After years of struggling to automate virtual machine deployment on other platforms, PowerShell and Hyper-V are a breath of fresh air. His passions include devops, Clojure (script), cooking, and natural languages.

Roy Verrips has been a system administrator since the mid-nineties for environments that include Novell NetWare, Linux/Unix, Microsoft Windows, and even OS X servers. Starting as far back as 2005, he grasped the advances in system administration that virtualizing allowed, and has since worked extensively on virtualizing servers and workstations using KEMU, VMware, KVM, VirtualBox, and Microsoft Hyper-V.

Roy's work has included virtualizing an OS X VDI environment (`http://www.aquaconnect.net/cs-united-christian-church-of-dubai`). In 2014, he received a CIO 50 award for virtualizing a luxury hotel's 18 physical servers down to a 3-node Hyper-V cluster (`http://www.cnmeonline.com/news/cio-50-awards-2014-full-list-of-winners`).

Roy wrote his first batch file when he was 9 years old and has been working in the field of command-line programming ever since, most recently using PowerShell extensively as his preferred utility language.

I'd like to thank my wife, Angela, for her love, ongoing support, encouragement, and never-ending patience. God has blessed me so richly with many things, that is, salvation, my wife, my children, and my Christian family. I'm nothing without any of these.

www.PacktPub.com

Support files, eBooks, discount offers, and more

For support files and downloads related to your book, please visit www.PacktPub.com.

Did you know that Packt offers eBook versions of every book published, with PDF and ePub files available? You can upgrade to the eBook version at www.PacktPub.com and as a print book customer, you are entitled to a discount on the eBook copy. Get in touch with us at service@packtpub.com for more details.

At www.PacktPub.com, you can also read a collection of free technical articles, sign up for a range of free newsletters and receive exclusive discounts and offers on Packt books and eBooks.

https://www2.packtpub.com/books/subscription/packtlib

Do you need instant solutions to your IT questions? PacktLib is Packt's online digital book library. Here, you can search, access, and read Packt's entire library of books.

Why subscribe?

- Fully searchable across every book published by Packt
- Copy and paste, print, and bookmark content
- On demand and accessible via a web browser

Free access for Packt account holders

If you have an account with Packt at www.PacktPub.com, you can use this to access PacktLib today and view 9 entirely free books. Simply use your login credentials for immediate access.

Instant updates on new Packt books

Get notified! Find out when new books are published by following @PacktEnterprise on Twitter or the *Packt Enterprise* Facebook page.

Table of Contents

Preface

Microsoft Hyper-V PowerShell Automation comes with a set of real-world scenarios and detailed scripts that will help you get started with PowerShell for Hyper-V and learn what administrative tasks you can do with PowerShell.

This book starts with the essential topics relating to PowerShell and then introduces the new features in Hyper-V version 3.0. This book explores the cmdlets in Hyper-V version 3.0 that can be used to manage and automate all configuration activities for managing the Hyper-V environment. The cmdlets are executed across the network using Windows Remote Management.

This book goes in depth and looks at the new features that are made available with Hyper-V version 3.0, and breaks down the mystery and confusion that surrounds which feature to use when. It also teaches you the PowerShell way to automate the usage of these features.

What this book covers

Chapter 1, New PowerShell Cmdlets in Hyper-V on Windows Server 2012 R2, explores the new features in Hyper-V Windows Server 2012 R2 and the associated cmdlets to manage these features.

Chapter 2, Managing Your Hyper-V Virtual Infrastructure, explores in depth the cmdlets that are available in the Hyper-V PowerShell module. This also covers cmdlets to manage properties of Hyper-V hosts, associated virtual machines, and virtual hard disks.

Chapter 3, Managing Your Hyper-V Virtual Machines, covers cmdlets to manage virtual switches, virtual machine migrations, snapshots, and also Hyper-V Replica.

Chapter 4, Creating Reusable PowerShell Scripts Using Hyper-V PowerShell Module Cmdlets, takes a deep dive into how to approach various complex administrative tasks and explores solutions for them by developing PowerShell scripts based on the Hyper-V PowerShell module.

Chapter 5, The Next Step – Integration with SCVMM, explores the advantages of integrating Hyper-V with SCVMM and the additional Hyper-V cmdlets that come with SCVMM.

Chapter 6, Troubleshooting Hyper-V Environment Issues and Best Practices Using PowerShell, explores the PowerShell way to troubleshoot a Hyper-V deployment. It also looks at the BPA Hyper-V module that helps to make sure that Hyper-V is deployed as per the best practices recommended by Microsoft.

What you need for this book

This book requires that you have Windows PowerShell 3.0, which is available out of the box in Windows Server 2012 and Windows Server 2012 R2. The latter has the Hyper-V role enabled on it. Windows PowerShell 3.0 is also available for earlier versions of Windows as part of Microsoft's Windows Management Framework 3.0. You should also have System Center Virtual Machine Manager 2012 and Windows Server 2012 R2 with you.

Who this book is for

This book is great for administrators who are new to automating Hyper-V administrative tasks using PowerShell. If you are familiar with the PowerShell command line and have some experience with the Windows Server, this book is perfect for you.

Conventions

In this book, you will find a number of text styles that distinguish between different kinds of information. Here are some examples of these styles and an explanation of their meaning.

Code words in text, database table names, folder names, filenames, file extensions, pathnames, dummy URLs, user input, and Twitter handles are shown as follows: "Let's look at the ways you can automate and manage your shared `.vhdx` guest clustering configuration using PowerShell."

A block of code is set as follows:

```
$Guid = [System.Guid]::NewGuid()
Set-SCCloud -JobGroup $Guid
$HostGroup = Get-SCVMHostGroup -Name "HostGroup02"
New-SCCloud -JobGroup $Guid -Name "Cloud02" -VMHostGroup
    $HostGroup -Description "This is a cloud for HostGroup02"
```

Any command-line input or output is written as follows:

```
Copy-VMFile "Fileserver_VM1" -SourcePath "D:\Test.txt" -
  DestinationPath "C:\Temp\Test.txt" -CreateFullPath -FileSource Host
```

New terms and **important words** are shown in bold. Words that you see on the screen, for example, in menus or dialog boxes, appear in the text like this: "Next, click on **Shrink**."

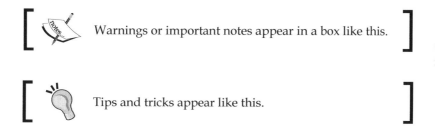

> Warnings or important notes appear in a box like this.

> Tips and tricks appear like this.

Reader feedback

Feedback from our readers is always welcome. Let us know what you think about this book—what you liked or disliked. Reader feedback is important for us as it helps us develop titles that you will really get the most out of.

To send us general feedback, simply e-mail feedback@packtpub.com, and mention the book's title in the subject of your message.

If there is a topic that you have expertise in and you are interested in either writing or contributing to a book, see our author guide at www.packtpub.com/authors.

Customer support

Now that you are the proud owner of a Packt book, we have a number of things to help you to get the most from your purchase.

Errata

Although we have taken every care to ensure the accuracy of our content, mistakes do happen. If you find a mistake in one of our books—maybe a mistake in the text or the code—we would be grateful if you could report this to us. By doing so, you can save other readers from frustration and help us improve subsequent versions of this book. If you find any errata, please report them by visiting http://www.packtpub. com/submit-errata, selecting your book, clicking on the **Errata Submission Form** link, and entering the details of your errata. Once your errata are verified, your submission will be accepted and the errata will be uploaded to our website or added to any list of existing errata under the Errata section of that title.

To view the previously submitted errata, go to https://www.packtpub.com/books/ content/support and enter the name of the book in the search field. The required information will appear under the **Errata** section.

Piracy

Piracy of copyrighted material on the Internet is an ongoing problem across all media. At Packt, we take the protection of our copyright and licenses very seriously. If you come across any illegal copies of our works in any form on the Internet, please provide us with the location address or website name immediately so that we can pursue a remedy.

Please contact us at copyright@packtpub.com with a link to the suspected pirated material.

We appreciate your help in protecting our authors and our ability to bring you valuable content.

Questions

If you have a problem with any aspect of this book, you can contact us at questions@packtpub.com, and we will do our best to address the problem.

1
New PowerShell Cmdlets in Hyper-V on Windows Server 2012 R2

The Hyper-V PowerShell module includes several significant features that extend its use, improve its usability, and allow you to control and manage your Hyper-V environment with more granular control.

Various organizations have moved on from Hyper-V (V2) to Hyper-V (V3). In Hyper-V (V2), the Hyper-V management shell was not built-in and the PowerShell module had to be manually installed. In Hyper-V (V3), Microsoft has provided an exhaustive set of cmdlets that can be used to manage and automate all configuration activities of the Hyper-V environment. The cmdlets are executed across the network using Windows Remote Management.

In this chapter, we will cover:

- The basics of setting up a Hyper-V environment using PowerShell
- The fundamental concepts of Hyper-V management with the Hyper-V management shell
- The updated features in Hyper-V

Here is a list of all the new features introduced in Hyper-V in Windows Server 2012 R2. We will be going in depth through the important changes that have come into the Hyper-V PowerShell module with the following features and functions:

- Shared virtual hard disk
- Resizing the live virtual hard disk
- Installing and configuring your Hyper-V environment

Installing and configuring Hyper-V using PowerShell

Before you proceed with the installation and configuration of Hyper-V, there are some prerequisites that need to be taken care of:

- The user account that is used to install the Hyper-V role should have administrative privileges on the computer

- There should be enough RAM on the server to run newly created virtual machines

Once the prerequisites have been taken care of, let's start with installing the Hyper-V role:

1. Open a PowerShell prompt in **Run as Administrator** mode:

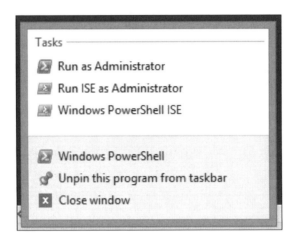

2. Type the following into the PowerShell prompt to install the Hyper-V role along with the management tools; once the installation is complete, the Hyper-V Server will reboot and the Hyper-V role will be successfully installed:

    ```
    Install-WindowsFeature –Name Hyper-V -IncludeManagementTools -
      Restart
    ```

3. Once the server boots up, verify the installation of Hyper-V using the Get-WindowsFeature cmdlet:

    ```
    Get-WindowsFeature -Name hyper*
    ```

You will be able to see that the Hyper-V role, Hyper-V PowerShell management shell, and the GUI management tools are successfully installed:

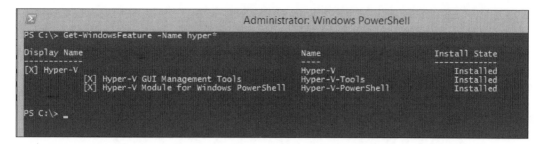

Fundamental concepts of Hyper-V management with the Hyper-V management shell

In this section, we will look at some of the fundamental concepts of Hyper-V management with the Hyper-V management shell. Once you get the Hyper-V role installed as per the steps illustrated in the previous section, a PowerShell module to manage your Hyper-V environment will also get installed. Now, perform the following steps:

1. Open a PowerShell prompt in the **Run as Administrator** mode.

2. PowerShell uses cmdlets that are built using a *verb-noun* naming system (for more details, refer to *Learning Windows PowerShell Names* at http://technet.microsoft.com/en-us/library/dd315315.aspx). Type the following command into the PowerShell prompt to get a list of all the cmdlets in the Hyper-V PowerShell module:

```
Get-Command -Module Hyper-V
```

Hyper-V in Windows Server 2012 R2 ships with about 178 cmdlets. These cmdlets allow a Hyper-V administrator to handle very simple, basic tasks to advanced ones such as setting up a Hyper-V replica for virtual machine disaster recovery.

3. To get the count of all the available Hyper-V cmdlets, you can type the following command in PowerShell:

```
Get-Command -Module Hyper-V | Measure-Object
```

The Hyper-V PowerShell cmdlets follow a very simple approach and are very user friendly. The cmdlet name itself indirectly communicates with the Hyper-V administrator about its functionality. The following screenshot shows the output of the Get command:

```
PS C:\> Get-Command -Module Hyper-V | Measure-Object


Count    : 178
Average  :
Sum      :
Maximum  :
Minimum  :
Property :


PS C:\>
```

For example, in the following screenshot, the Remove-VMSwitch cmdlet itself says that it's used to delete a previously created virtual machine switch:

```
Cmdlet          Remove-VMSnapshot                           Hyper-V
Cmdlet          Remove-VMStoragePath                        Hyper-V
Cmdlet          Remove-VMSwitch                             Hyper-V
Cmdlet          Remove-VMSwitchExtensionPortFeature         Hyper-V
Cmdlet          Remove-VMSwitchExtensionSwitchFeature       Hyper-V
```

4. If the administrator is still not sure about the task that can be performed by the cmdlet, he or she can get help with detailed examples using the Get-Help cmdlet. To get help on the cmdlet type, type the cmdlet name in the prescribed format. To make sure that the latest version of help files are installed on the server, run the Update-Help cmdlet before executing the following cmdlet:

```
Get-Help <Hyper-V cmdlet> -Full
```

The following screenshot is an example of the Get-Help cmdlet:

```
PS C:\> Get-Help Resize-VHD -full

NAME
    Resize-VHD

SYNOPSIS
    Resizes a virtual hard disk.

SYNTAX
    Resize-VHD [-Path] <String[]> [-SizeBytes] <UInt64> [-AsJob] [-ComputerName <String[
    atIf] [<CommonParameters>]

    Resize-VHD [-Path] <String[]> [-AsJob] [-ComputerName <String[]>] [-Passthru] -ToMin
    <CommonParameters>]

DESCRIPTION
    The Resize-VHD cmdlet resizes a virtual hard disk. This cmdlet lets you shrink or ex
     disk, but the shrink operation is allowed only on VHDX virtual hard disks. The shri
    shrink the virtual disk to less than its minimum size (available through the VHDX ob

    Resize-VHD is an offline operation; the virtual hard disk must not be attached when

PARAMETERS
    -AsJob [<SwitchParameter>]
        Specifies that the cmdlet is to be run as a background job.

        Required?                false
        Position?                named
        Default value
        Accept pipeline input?   false
        Accept wildcard characters? false

    -ComputerName <String[]>
        Specifies one or more Hyper-V hosts on which a virtual hard disk is to be resize
         and fully-qualified domain names are allowable. The default is the local comput
        ".") to specify the local computer explicitly.
```

Shared virtual hard disks

This new and improved feature in Windows Server 2012 R2 allows an administrator to share a virtual hard disk file (the .vhdx file format) between multiple virtual machines. These .vhdx files can be used as shared storage for a failover cluster created between virtual machines (also known as guest clustering). A shared virtual hard disk allows you to create data disks and witness disks using .vhdx files with some advantages:

- Shared disks are ideal for SQL database files and file servers
- Shared disks can be run on generation 1 and generation 2 virtual machines

This new feature allows you to save on storage costs and use the `.vhdx` files for guest clustering, enabling easier deployment rather than using virtual Fibre Channel or **Internet Small Computer System Interface (iSCSI)**, which are complicated and require storage configuration changes such as zoning and **Logic Unit Number (LUN)** masking.

In Windows Server 2012 R2, virtual iSCSI disks (both shared and unshared virtual hard disk files) show up as virtual SAS disks when you add an iSCSI hard disk to a virtual machine. Shared virtual hard disks (`.vhdx`) files can be placed on **Cluster Shared Volumes (CSV)** or a Scale-Out File Server cluster

Let's look at the ways you can automate and manage your shared `.vhdx` guest clustering configuration using PowerShell. In the following example, we will demonstrate how you can create a two-node file server cluster using the shared VHDX feature. After that, let's set up a testing environment within which we can start learning these new features. The steps are as follows:

1. We will start by creating two virtual machines each with 50 GB OS drives, which contains a sysprep image of Windows Server 2012 R2. Each virtual machine will have 4 GB RAM and four virtual CPUs.

 `D:\vhd\base_1.vhdx` and `D:\vhd\base_2.vhdx` are already existing VHDX files with sysprepped image of Windows Server 2012 R2.

The following code is used to create two virtual machines:

```
New-VM -Name "Fileserver_VM1" -MemoryStartupBytes 4GB -
    NewVHDPath d:\vhd\base_1.vhdx -NewVHDSizeBytes 50GB


New-VM -Name "Fileserver_VM2" -MemoryStartupBytes 4GB -
    NewVHDPath d:\vhd\base_2.vhdx -NewVHDSizeBytes 50GB
```

2. Next, we will install the file server role and configure a failover cluster on both the virtual machines using PowerShell.

 You need to enable PowerShell remoting on both the file servers and also have them joined to a domain.

The following is the code:

```
Install-WindowsFeature -computername Fileserver_VM1 File-
    Services, FS-FileServer, Failover-Clustering


Install-WindowsFeature -computername Fileserver_VM1 RSAT-
    Clustering –IncludeAllSubFeature


Install-WindowsFeature -computername Fileserver_VM2 File-
    Services, FS-FileServer, Failover-Clustering


Install-WindowsFeature -computername Fileserver_VM2 RSAT-
    Clustering -IncludeAllSubFeature
```

3. Once we have the virtual machines created and the file server and failover clustering features installed, we will create the failover cluster as per Microsoft's best practices using the following set of cmdlets:

```
New-Cluster -Name Cluster1 -Node FileServer_VM1,
    FileServer_VM2 -StaticAddress 10.0.0.59 -NoStorage –
    Verbose
```

You will need to choose a name and IP address that fits your organization.

4. Next, we will create two vhdx files named sharedvhdx_data.vhdx (which will be used as a data disk) and sharedvhdx_quorum.vhdx (which will be used as the quorum or the witness disk). To do this, the following commands need to be run on the Hyper-V cluster:

```
New-VHD -Path
    c:\ClusterStorage\Volume1\sharedvhdx_data.VHDX -Fixed -
    SizeBytes 10GB


New-VHD -Path
    c:\ClusterStorage\Volume1\sharedvhdx_quorum.VHDX -Fixed -
    SizeBytes 1GB
```

5. Once we have created these virtual hard disk files, we will add them as shared `.vhdx` files. We will attach these newly created VHDX files to the `Fileserver_VM1` and `Fileserver_VM2` virtual machines and specify the parameter-shared VHDX files for guest clustering:

```
Add-VMHardDiskDrive -VMName Fileserver_VM1 -Path
  c:\ClusterStorage\Volume1\sharedvhdx_data.VHDX -
  ShareVirtualDisk
```

```
Add-VMHardDiskDrive -VMName Fileserver_VM2 -Path
  c:\ClusterStorage\Volume1\sharedvhdx_data.VHDX -
  ShareVirtualDisk
```

6. Finally, we will be making the disks available online and adding them to the failover cluster using the following command:

```
Get-ClusterAvailableDisk | Add-ClusterDisk
```

Once we have executed the preceding set of steps, we will have a highly available file server infrastructure using shared VHD files.

Live virtual hard disk resizing

With Windows Server 2012 R2, a newly added feature in Hyper-V allows the administrators to expand or shrink the size of a virtual hard disk attached to the SCSI controller while the virtual machines are still running. Hyper-V administrators can now perform maintenance operations on a live VHD and avoid any downtime by not temporarily shutting down the virtual machine for these maintenance activities.

Prior to Windows Server 2012 R2, to resize a VHD attached to the virtual machine, it had to be turned off leading to costly downtime. Using the GUI controls, the VHD resize can be done by using only the **Edit Virtual Hard Disk** wizard. Also, note that the VHDs that were previously expanded can be shrunk.

The Windows PowerShell way of doing a VHD resize is by using the `Resize-VirtualDisk` cmdlet. Let's look at the ways you can automate a VHD resize using PowerShell. In the next example, we will demonstrate how you can expand and shrink a virtual hard disk connected to a VM's SCSI controller. We will continue using the virtual machine that we created for our previous example. We have a pre-created VHD of 50 GB that is connected to the virtual machine's SCSI controller.

Expanding the virtual hard disk

Let's resize the aforementioned virtual hard disk to 57 GB using the
`Resize-Virtualdisk` cmdlet:

```
Resize-VirtualDisk -Name "scsidisk" -Size (57GB)
```

Next, if we open the VM settings and perform an inspect disk operation, we'll be able
to see that the VHDX file size has become 57 GB:

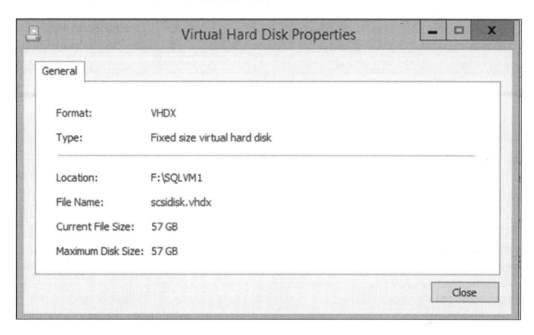

Also, one can verify this when he or she logs into the VM, opens disk management,
and extends the unused partition. You can see that the disk size has increased to 57GB:

Resizing the virtual hard disk

Let's resize the earlier mentioned VHD to 57 GB using the `Resize-Virtualdisk` cmdlet:

1. For this exercise, the primary requirement is to shrink the disk partition by logging in to the VM using disk management, as you can see in the following screenshot; we're shrinking the VHDX file by 7 GB:

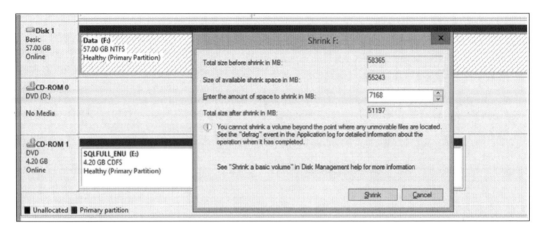

2. Next, click on **Shrink**. Once you complete this step, you will see that the unallocated space is 7 GB. You can also execute this step using the `Resize-Partition` PowerShell cmdlet:

   ```
   Get-Partition -DiskNumber 1 | Resize-Partition -Size 50GB
   ```

   The following screenshot shows the partition:

3. Next, we will resize/shrink the VHD to 50 GB:

   ```
   Resize-VirtualDisk -Name "scsidisk" -Size (50GB)
   ```

Once the previous steps have been executed successfully, run a re-scan disk using disk management and you will see that the disk size is 50GB:

The storage quality of the service feature

The storage **quality of service (QoS)** feature in Windows Server 2012 R2 allows us to set a specific level of I/O throughput for virtual machines. This is best done on virtual machines that are resource-hungry. You can effectively set an automatic hard cap by specifying the maximum **input/output operations per second (IOPS)** for a virtual hard disk associated with a particular virtual machine.

This allows the administrator to set a throttle limit on the IOPS consumed by a virtual machine, thereby controlling it from consuming resources of other virtual machines. So, let me show you an example on how you can set the storage level QoS for the virtual machine. We will be using the sample virtual machine that we used for our previous example, by making use of the following code:

```
Get-VM Fileserver_VM1| Get-VMHardDiskDrive -ControllerType SCSI |
  Set-VMHardDiskDrive -MaximumIOPS 100 -MinimumIOPS 2
```

As you can see in the previous example, we get the virtual machine properties for `FileServer_VM1` or `FileServer_VM2` using `Get-VM`. Next, we get the VHD drives attached to the SCSI controller on the virtual machine using `Get-vmharddiskdrive`. Finally, we set the maximum and minimum IOPs for the virtual machine using the `set-vmharddiskdrive` cmdlet.

Once we execute this cmdlet on a PowerShell prompt, we are able to see that the QoS properties for the VM have been modified:

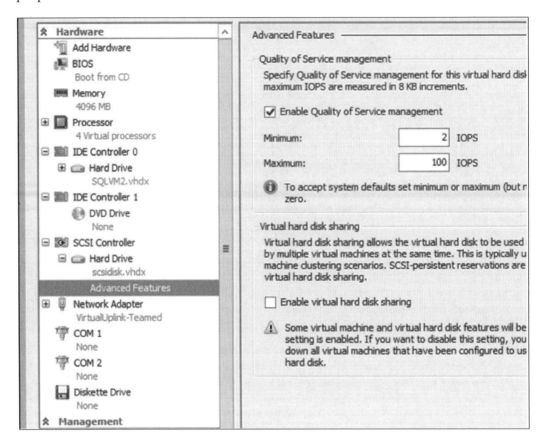

Virtual machine generation

With the introduction of the concept of virtual machine generation in Windows Server 2012 R2, the virtual machines have been classified broadly into two generations: generation 1 and generation 2. Generation 1 VMs can boot only from a disk attached to the IDE controller or network boot from a legacy network adapter. In addition, the boot configurations are taken care by BIOS. Generation 2 virtual machines are UEFI-based, which gives us features like secure boot; it allows us to boot the virtual machines from the SCSI disk and there is no requirement for an IDE controller-based boot method. Also, it allows network boot over the synthetic network adapter. Generation 2 virtual machines are UEFI based; this feature is supported only on windows 2012 or later versions and only on 64-bit operating systems. The boot time in generation 2 virtual machines is quicker than generation 1 virtual machines.

Creating either generation 1 or generation 2 virtual machines is very simple with PowerShell. You just need to specify an integer value for the generation parameter. The following examples show how you can go about doing this:

- To create a generation 1 virtual machine, you can specify the generation type as 1, as shown in the following example:

```
New-VM -Name "new 3" -MemoryStartupBytes 1GB -VHDPath
  d:\vhd\BaseImage.vhdx -Generation 1
```

 For these examples, you have the `BaseImage.vhdx` file placed at `d:\vhd`.

- Similarly, to create a generation 2 virtual machine, you can specify the generation type as 2, as shown in the following example:

```
New-VM -Name "new 3" -MemoryStartupBytes 1GB -VHDPath
  d:\vhd\BaseImage.vhdx -Generation 2
```

Updated features in integration services

The newly updated integration services in Hyper-V allow the administrator to copy a file to a VM without shutting it down and also without accessing a network. For this feature to work, the `Guest Services` feature needs to be enabled on a virtual machine's integration services properties; this feature is disabled by default and can be enabled on virtual machines using the `Enable-VMIntegrationService` Windows PowerShell cmdlet. The following command shows how you can enable this feature on a virtual machine:

```
Enable-VMIntegrationService -Name "Guest Service Interface" -
  VMName Fileserver_VM1
```

Once this feature is enabled, you can use the `Copy-VMFile` cmdlet to copy files to a virtual machine. The following command shows how you can use this cmdlet to copy files to a virtual machine:

```
Copy-VMFile "Fileserver_VM1" -SourcePath "D:\Test.txt" -
  DestinationPath "C:\Temp\Test.txt" -CreateFullPath -FileSource Host
```

Updated features for exporting a virtual machine

With the updated Hyper-V features in Windows Server 2012 R2, you can export a live VM and its snapshot without shutting down the VM, which had to be done in Windows 2012. This helps the administrator to avoid unnecessary downtime for the virtual machine export. There are two cmdlets that can be used for the live export of virtual machines and its snapshots; these are the `Export-VM` and the `Export-VMSnapshot` cmdlets.

The `Export-VM` cmdlet exports a virtual machine to disk. This cmdlet creates a folder at a specified location with three subfolders: `Snapshots`, `Virtual Hard Disks`, and `Virtual Machines`. The `Snapshots` and `Virtual Hard Disks` folders contain the snapshots and the VHDs of the specified virtual machine respectively. The `Virtual Machines` folder contains the configuration XML of the specified virtual machine. The following command exports all virtual machines to root of the `D` drive. Each virtual machine will be exported to its own folder:

```
Get-VM | Export-VM –Path D:\
```

The export of a live VM is very different from the export of a snapshot of a live VM. The export of a live VM can be done by creating a snapshot first, then exporting it, and then finally removing the snapshot. The following cmdlet shows you how to do this:

```
Get-VM | Checkpoint-VM| Export-VMSnapshot -path d:\ | Remove-VMSnapshot
```

The `Export-VMSnapshot` cmdlet exports a virtual machine snapshot to disk:

```
PS C:\>Export-VMSnapshot –Name 'Base Image' –VMName TestVM –Path D:\
```

The preceding command exports the `Base Image` snapshot of the `TestVM` virtual machine to `D:\`.

Updated features in Hyper-V Replica

Windows Server 2012 R2 brings in new and updated features to Hyper-V Replica called extended replication, which allows the replica information from the primary site to be sent to a third extended replica server that will be used to further business continuity protection. Also, there is an addition of the feature that allows us to configure the frequency of replication, which was previously a fixed value. Hyper-V Replica provides a comprehensive disaster recovery solution for the Hyper-V infrastructure.

The Hyper-V Replica feature in Windows Server 2012 R2 allows you to configure replication intervals to three intervals: 30 seconds, 5 minutes, and 15 minutes. In Windows Server 2012, it was hardcoded to a 5 minute interval.

The concept of extended replica allows you to send an additional copy of the VM to an extended replica server. This allows a VM copy to be present in three or more separate locations, which allows us to keep multiple copies of the virtual machines that are mission-critical. When you create an extended replica of a virtual machine, it can be kept at either 5 minutes or 15 minutes.

The following syntax can be used to configure Hyper-V. Here, we use the `Enable-VMReplication` cmdlet to enable replication of a `VM` `VM01` virtual machine onto an extended replica Hyper-v server called `HYPERVSERVER3` on a replication server port of `80` with the replication frequency of 300 seconds (5 minutes):

```
Enable-VMReplication -VMName VM01 -ReplicaServerName HYPERVSERVER3
  -ReplicaServerPort 80 -AuthenticationType Kerberos -
  ReplicationFrequencySec 300
```

Summary

In this chapter, we went through the basics of setting up a Hyper-V environment using PowerShell. We also explored the fundamental concepts of Hyper-V management with Hyper-V management shell.

In the next chapter, we will be covering the installation and configuration of your Hyper-V environment on a Windows Server 2012 R2 environment using PowerShell. Also, we will learn how to set up your PowerShell environment to get started using the Hyper-V management shell.

2
Managing Your Hyper-V Virtual Infrastructure

Managing Hyper-V virtual infrastructure components is an integral part of a Hyper-V administrator's day-to-day activities. Performing these administrative tasks manually is time-consuming and leads to a reduction in productivity; replacing these repetitive tasks with PowerShell leads to better consistency (no typos or execution of incorrect tasks). This also helps a senior administrator delegate these tasks to other members in the team and audit the tasks performed by those individuals so that he or she can concentrate on other important tasks that lead to a better learning curve and improve the creative ability of the administrator to automate complex tasks.

In the current chapter and *Chapter 3*, *Managing Your Hyper-V Virtual Machines*, we will explore the various PowerShell cmdlets in depth that can be used to automate these set of repetitive tasks performed by an administrator.

In this chapter, we will cover the following:

- Extracting information about Hyper-V hosts and the associated virtual machines
- Creating, deleting, starting, and stopping virtual machines
- Configuring properties on virtual machines

Extracting information about Hyper-V hosts and the associated virtual machines

Microsoft offers the ability to extract information related to the Hyper-V infrastructure using PowerShell. It is now possible to perform virtual machine management from the command line using the Hyper-V PowerShell module.

Let's start exploring the ways in which you can extract information related to a Hyper-V host.

For Hyper-V deployments that are not clustered, host-level information can be extracted by the `Get-VMHost` cmdlet:

```
Get-VMHost | fl *
```

Open up a PowerShell prompt in your Windows Server 2012 R2 Hyper-V server in the **Run as Administrator** mode and type the following cmdlets:

- `Get-ClusterNode`: This cmdlet shows details of the nodes in the cluster
- `Get-ClusterNode | select @{l='ComputerName';e={$_.name}}`: This cmdlet shows the names of the Hyper-V hosts in the cluster
- `Get-VMHost -computername <HVHostName>`: This cmdlet shows details of the Hyper-V hosts

Now, by combining all the preceding cmdlets together, we can extract host-level information:

```
Get-ClusterNode | select @{l='ComputerName';e={$_.name}} |
  Get-VMHost | fl *
```

As you can see in the preceding command, we used the `Get-ClusterNode` cmdlet to first get a list of all the nodes in the Hyper-V cluster. Next, we created a custom property for `computername` and passed it to the `Get-VMHost` cmdlet to extract information about all the Hyper-V hosts in the cluster.

Once you type the cmdlet, you will be able to see lots of details regarding the host. If you were to do this manually, it would need you to open up a GUI and access the console properties one by one and extract the required information. The following screenshot shows details with respect to the host:

```
PS C:\> Get-ClusterNode

Name             ID    State
----             --    -----
hyperv01         2     Up
hyperv02         1     Up


PS C:\> Get-ClusterNode | select @{l='ComputerName';e={$_.name}} | Get-VMHost | fl *

ComputerName                             : hyperv01
VirtualHardDiskPath                      : C:\Users\Public\Documents\Hyper-V\Virtual Hard Disks
VirtualMachinePath                       : C:\ProgramData\Microsoft\Windows\Hyper-V
FullyQualifiedDomainName                 : virtualcloud.com
Name                                     : hyperv01
MacAddressMinimum                        : 00155D8BBB000
MacAddressMaximum                        : 00155D8BBB0FF
MaximumStorageMigrations                 : 2
MaximumVirtualMachineMigrations          : 2
VirtualMachineMigrationEnabled           : True
VirtualMachineMigrationAuthenticationType : CredSSP
VirtualMachineMigrationPerformanceOption : Compression
UseAnyNetworkForMigration                : False
FibreChannelWwnn                         : C003FF0000FFFF00
FibreChannelWwpnMaximum                  : C003FFEEE06EFFFF
FibreChannelWwpnMinimum                  : C003FFEEE06E0000
LogicalProcessorCount                    : 24
MemoryCapacity                           : 60100444160
ResourceMeteringSaveInterval             : 01:00:00
NumaSpanningEnabled                      : True
EnableEnhancedSessionMode                : False
HostNumaStatus                           : {hyperv01, hyperv01}
NumaStatus                               :
InternalNetworkAdapters                  : {}
ExternalNetworkAdapters                  : {}
IovSupport                               : False
IovSupportReasons                        : {This system has a security vulnerability in the system I/O remapping
                                           hardware. As a precaution, the ability to use SR-IOV has been disabled.
                                           You should contact your system manufacturer for an updated BIOS which
                                           enables Root Port Alternate Error Delivery mechanism. If all Virtual
                                           Machines intended to use SR-IOV run trusted workloads, SR-IOV may be
                                           enabled by adding a registry key of type DwORD with value 1 named
```

As you can see in the preceding screenshot, we get the default virtual machine disk and machine path, properties for virtual machine migrations, the processor count, host memory size, and even detailed properties on network adapters and the status of NUMA.

You might have noticed that some of the properties that relate to the NUMA node and network adapters appear in curly braces. This indicates that there are subproperties inside them and you can extract this information by expanding their properties.

Let's explore these properties using the expandproperty parameter in the select-object cmdlet.

Type the next set of cmdlets in the PowerShell prompt to extract details of the Hyper-V host NUMA node:

Get-VMHost | select -ExpandProperty hostnumastatus

The following screenshot shows the output:

```
PS C:\> Get-VMHost | select -ExpandProperty hostnumastatus

NodeId                 : 0
ProcessorsAvailability : {0, 0, 0, 0...}
MemoryAvailable        : 6439
MemoryTotal            : 24548
ComputerName           : HYPERV01

NodeId                 : 1
ProcessorsAvailability : {0, 0, 0, 0...}
MemoryAvailable        : 8596
MemoryTotal            : 32768
ComputerName           : HYPERV01
```

You can also extract the information seen in the preceding screenshot using the
Get-VMHostNumaNode cmdlet:

```
Get-ClusterNode | select @{l='ComputerName';e={$_.name}} |
  Get-VMHostNumaNode | fl *
```

```
PS C:\> Get-ClusterNode | select @{l='ComputerName';e={$_.name}} | Get-VMHostNumaNode | fl *

NodeId                 : 0
ProcessorsAvailability : {0, 0, 0, 0...}
MemoryAvailable        : 6439
MemoryTotal            : 24548
ComputerName           : hyperv01

NodeId                 : 1
ProcessorsAvailability : {0, 0, 0, 0...}
MemoryAvailable        : 8595
MemoryTotal            : 32768
ComputerName           : hyperv01

NodeId                 : 0
ProcessorsAvailability : {0, 0, 0, 0...}
MemoryAvailable        : 26601
MemoryTotal            : 32740
ComputerName           : hyperv02

NodeId                 : 1
ProcessorsAvailability : {0, 0, 0, 0...}
MemoryAvailable        : 26624
MemoryTotal            : 32768
ComputerName           : hyperv02
```

Next, let's extract information about the internal and external network adapters
of the Hyper-V hosts using the technique shown in the previous example:

```
Get-VMHost | select -ExpandProperty InternalNetworkAdapters | fl *
```

```
PS C:\Users\Administrator> Get-VMHost | select -ExpandProperty InternalNetworkAdapters | fl *

IsManagementOs            : True
DeviceId                  : {B91E6037-46DD-4934-8AFC-0D13EB363623}
Name                      : VirtualUplink-Teamed
MandatoryFeatureId        :
IsLegacy                  : False
IsExternalAdapter         : False
Id                        : Microsoft:21A0D908-39AC-4872-AADF-A7F261B53C15\FCF34438-A0C3-46E0-ASCF-B3EA86A3791F
AdapterId                 : E5AB2972-1988-4657-BD06-EF79858A3110
DynamicMacAddressEnabled  : False
MacAddress                : 001999C9E215
MacAddressSpoofing        : Off
SwitchId                  : 21a0d908-39ac-4872-aadf-a7f261b53c15
Connected                 : True
PoolName                  :
SwitchName                : VirtualUplink-Teamed
AclList                   : {}
ExtendedAclList           : {}
IsolationSetting          : Microsoft.HyperV.PowerShell.VMNetworkAdapterIsolationSetting
CurrentIsolationMode      : Vlan
RoutingDomainList         : {}
DhcpGuard                 : Off
RouterGuard               : Off
PortMirroringMode         : None
IeeePriorityTag           : Off
VirtualSubnetId           : 0
DynamicIPAddressLimit     : 0
StormLimit                : 0
AllowTeaming              : Off
VMQWeight                 : 100
IPsecOffloadMaxSA         : 512
VmqUsage                  : 0
IPsecOffloadSAUsage       : 0
VFDataPathActive          : False
VMQueue                   :
MandatoryFeatureName      :
VlanSetting               : Microsoft.HyperV.PowerShell.VMNetworkAdapterVlanSetting
BandwidthSetting          :
BandwidthPercentage       : 0
TestReplicaPoolName       :
TestReplicaSwitchName     :
```

Similarly, you can extract information about the external network adapters too using the following cmdlet:

```
Get-VMHost | select -ExpandProperty ExternalNetworkAdapters | fl *
```

```
PS C:\Users\Administrator> Get-VMHost | select -ExpandProperty ExternalNetworkAdapters | fl *

IsExternalAdapter         : True
Name                      : VirtualUplink-Teamed_External
MandatoryFeatureId        :
IsLegacy                  : False
IsManagementOs            : False
Id                        :
AdapterId                 : {834FAB96-99D9-42D3-80D6-8B0B0696655D}
DynamicMacAddressEnabled  : False
MacAddress                :
MacAddressSpoofing        : Off
SwitchId                  : 21a0d908-39ac-4872-aadf-a7f261b53c15
Connected                 : True
PoolName                  :
SwitchName                : VirtualUplink-Teamed
AclList                   : {}
ExtendedAclList           : {}
IsolationSetting          : Microsoft.HyperV.PowerShell.VMNetworkAdapterIsolationSetting
CurrentIsolationMode      : Vlan
RoutingDomainList         : {}
DhcpGuard                 : Off
RouterGuard               : Off
PortMirroringMode         : None
IeeePriorityTag           : Off
VirtualSubnetId           : 0
DynamicIPAddressLimit     : 0
StormLimit                : 0
AllowTeaming              : Off
vMQWeight                 : 0
IPsecOffloadMaxSA         :
VmqUsage                  : 0
IPsecOffloadSAUsage       : 0
VFDataPathActive          : False
VMQueue                   :
MandatoryFeatureName      :
VlanSetting               : Microsoft.HyperV.PowerShell.VMNetworkAdapterVlanSetting
BandwidthSetting          :
```

Likewise, we can also extract a variety of information about the virtual machines running on Hyper-V hosts.

Type the following cmdlet to extract the list of all the virtual machines that reside on Hyper-V cluster nodes:

```
Get-ClusterNode | select @{l='ComputerName';e={$_.name}} | %
  {Get-VM -ComputerName $_.computername}
```

```
PS C:\> Get-ClusterNode | select @{l='ComputerName';e={$_.name}} | % {Get-VM -ComputerName $_.computername}

Name  State   CPUUsage(%) MemoryAssigned(M) Uptime        Status
----  -----   ----------- ----------------- ------        ------
VM1   Running 0           726               18.23:49:15   Operating normally
VM10  Running 0           2048              18.23:50:20   Operating normally
VM11  Running 0           2048              18.23:08:07   Operating normally
VM12  Running 0           2048              18.23:08:16   Operating normally
VM13  Running 0           2048              18.23:08:26   Operating normally
VM14  Running 0           2048              18.23:08:27   Operating normally
VM15  Running 0           2048              18.23:06:28   Operating normally
VM16  Running 0           2048              18.23:06:45   Operating normally
VM17  Running 0           2048              18.23:08:19   Operating normally
VM18  Running 0           2048              18.23:08:18   Operating normally
VM2   Running 0           2048              18.23:50:07   Operating normally
VM20  Running 0           2048              18.23:08:17   Operating normally
VM21  Running 0           2048              18.05:05:17   Operating normally
VM4   Running 0           2048              18.23:50:21   Operating normally
VM7   Running 0           2048              18.23:50:22   Operating normally
VM8   Running 0           2048              18.23:50:22   Operating normally
VM9   Running 0           2048              18.23:50:16   Operating normally
VM19  Running 0           2048              18.04:40:21   Operating normally
VM6   Running 0           2048              18.21:21:30   Operating normally


PS C:\> _
```

You can also extract information about individual virtual machines using the following syntax. In the following example, I'll redirect the cmdlet towards a single virtual machine and extract information about it:

```
Get-VM <Virtual machine Name> | fl *
```

```
PS C:\Users\Administrator> Get-VM scvmm2012r2 | fl *

VMName                         : SCVMM2012R2
VMId                           : c0538366-6112-4f25-b403-1af94969a3b1
Id                             : c0538366-6112-4f25-b403-1af94969a3b1
Name                           : SCVMM2012R2
State                          : Running
IntegrationServicesState       : Update required
OperationalStatus              : {Ok}
PrimaryOperationalStatus       : Ok
SecondaryOperationalStatus     :
StatusDescriptions             : {Operating normally}
PrimaryStatusDescription       : Operating normally
SecondaryStatusDescription     :
Status                         : Operating normally
Heartbeat                      : OkApplicationsHealthy
ReplicationState               : Disabled
ReplicationHealth              : NotApplicable
ReplicationMode                : None
CPUUsage                       : 0
MemoryAssigned                 : 8589934592
MemoryDemand                   : 0
MemoryStatus                   :
SmartPagingFileInUse           : False
Uptime                         : 4.02:17:59
IntegrationServicesVersion     : 6.2.9200.16384
ResourceMeteringEnabled        : False
ConfigurationLocation          : G:\Vinith-SCVMM2012R2-VirtualCloud\SCVMM2012R2
SnapshotFileLocation           : G:\Vinith-SCVMM2012R2-VirtualCloud\SCVMM2012R2
AutomaticStartAction           : StartIfRunning
AutomaticStopAction            : Save
AutomaticStartDelay            : 0
SmartPagingFilePath            : G:\Vinith-SCVMM2012R2-VirtualCloud\SCVMM2012R2
NumaAligned                    : True
NumaNodesCount                 : 1
NumaSocketCount                : 1
Key                            : Microsoft.HyperV.PowerShell.VirtualMachineObjectKey
```

Similarly, there are other sets of cmdlets that can be used to extract information about a virtual machine, which includes its BIOS, DVD dive information, firmware, integration service, and so on.

To get a list of all the cmdlets that can be used to extract information about the Hyper-V infrastructure and that includes the virtual machines and the Hyper-V host, type the following cmdlet in the command line:

```
Get-Command get-vm*
```

PowerShell has an autocomplete feature; so if you type Get-VM and press *Tab*, it will rotate through the various autocomplete options. Also, note that after you select your desired cmdlet, pressing *Space*, then -, and then pressing *Tab* again will rotate through the parameters that are available:

```
PS C:\Users\Administrator> gcm get-vm*

CommandType     Name                                          ModuleName
-----------     ----                                          ----------
Cmdlet          Get-VM                                        Hyper-V
Cmdlet          Get-VMBios                                    Hyper-V
Cmdlet          Get-VMComPort                                 Hyper-V
Cmdlet          Get-VMConnectAccess                           Hyper-V
Cmdlet          Get-VMDvdDrive                                Hyper-V
Cmdlet          Get-VMFibreChannelHba                         Hyper-V
Cmdlet          Get-VMFirmware                                Hyper-V
Cmdlet          Get-VMFloppyDiskDrive                         Hyper-V
Cmdlet          Get-VMHardDiskDrive                           Hyper-V
Cmdlet          Get-VMHost                                    Hyper-V
Cmdlet          Get-VMHostNumaNode                            Hyper-V
Cmdlet          Get-VMHostNumaNodeStatus                      Hyper-V
Cmdlet          Get-VMIdeController                           Hyper-V
Cmdlet          Get-VMIntegrationService                      Hyper-V
Cmdlet          Get-VMMemory                                  Hyper-V
Cmdlet          Get-VMMigrationNetwork                        Hyper-V
Cmdlet          Get-VMNetworkAdapter                          Hyper-V
Cmdlet          Get-VMNetworkAdapterAcl                       Hyper-V
Cmdlet          Get-VMNetworkAdapterExtendedAcl               Hyper-V
Cmdlet          Get-VMNetworkAdapterFailoverConfiguration     Hyper-V
Cmdlet          Get-VmNetworkAdapterIsolation                 Hyper-V
Cmdlet          Get-VMNetworkAdapterRoutingDomainMapping      Hyper-V
Cmdlet          Get-VMNetworkAdapterVlan                      Hyper-V
Cmdlet          Get-VMProcessor                               Hyper-V
Cmdlet          Get-VMRemoteFx3dVideoAdapter                  Hyper-V
Cmdlet          Get-VMRemoteFXPhysicalVideoAdapter            Hyper-V
Cmdlet          Get-VMReplication                             Hyper-V
Cmdlet          Get-VMReplicationAuthorizationEntry           Hyper-V
Cmdlet          Get-VMReplicationServer                       Hyper-V
Cmdlet          Get-VMResourcePool                            Hyper-V
Cmdlet          Get-VMSan                                     Hyper-V
Cmdlet          Get-VMScsiController                          Hyper-V
Cmdlet          Get-VMsFromBackup                             SMHV
Cmdlet          Get-VMSnapshot                                Hyper-V
Cmdlet          Get-VMStoragePath                             Hyper-V
Cmdlet          Get-VMSwitch                                  Hyper-V
Cmdlet          Get-VMSwitchExtension                         Hyper-V
Cmdlet          Get-VMSwitchExtensionPortData                 Hyper-V
Cmdlet          Get-VMSwitchExtensionPortFeature              Hyper-V
Cmdlet          Get-VMSwitchExtensionSwitchData               Hyper-V
Cmdlet          Get-VMSwitchExtensionSwitchFeature            Hyper-V
Cmdlet          Get-VMSystemSwitchExtension                   Hyper-V
Cmdlet          Get-VMSystemSwitchExtensionPortFeature        Hyper-V
Cmdlet          Get-VMSystemSwitchExtensionSwitchFeature      Hyper-V
```

Creating, deleting, starting, and stopping virtual machines

Creating, deleting, starting, or stopping a virtual machine is one of the most repetitive tasks that a Hyper-V administrator needs to perform, but with PowerShell, all these tasks can be scripted and made simpler to execute.

Creating a virtual machine

Creating a virtual machine is relatively simple with PowerShell using the New-VM PowerShell cmdlet. Before you execute the commands to create a VM, let's look at Get-VM, which gives the list of all the VMs that are present on the Hyper-V host cluster. The following command gets the nodes that are part of the Hyper-V cluster. It creates a value by property and name called ComputerName and passes it to the Get-VM cmdlet:

```
Get-ClusterNode | select @{l='ComputerName';e={$_.name}} | Get-VM
```

Windows Server 2012 R2 introduced the concept of generation 1 and generation 2 virtual machines, and the same can be created with PowerShell:

Then, we use the New-VM cmdlet to create virtual machines with the prefix VMtest followed by the Hyper-V hostname, which comes from the pipeline. The following example gets the details of all the nodes of the Hyper-V cluster:

```
Get-ClusterNode | select @{l='ComputerName';e={$_.name}} | %
  {New-VM -Name VMtest$($_.computername) -
  Generation 2 -MemoryStartupBytes 2GB -ComputerName $_.computername
  }
```

The following screenshot illustrates the output of the preceding command:

```
PS C:\> Get-ClusterNode | select @{l='ComputerName';e={$_.name}} | % {New-VM -Name VMtest$($_.computername) -Generation
2 -MemoryStartupBytes 2GB -ComputerName $_.computername }

Name            State CPUUsage(%) MemoryAssigned(M) Uptime    Status
----            ----- ----------- ----------------- ------    ------
VMtesthyperv01  Off   0           0                 00:00:00  Operating normally
VMtesthyperv02  Off   0           0                 00:00:00  Operating normally
```

As you can see in the preceding example, I created two virtual machines, vmtesthyperv01 and vmtresthyperv02, on both the nodes of the Hyper-V cluster. The New-VM cmdlet accepts different parameters and can be customized based on user needs. For more details on the New-VM cmdlet, explore detailed examples using the following syntax:

Get-Help New-VM -Examples

```
PS C:\Users\Administrator> Get-Help New-VM -Examples
NAME
    New-VM

SYNOPSIS
    Creates a new virtual machine.

    Example 1

    PS C:\> New-VM -Name "new 1" -MemoryStartupBytes 512MB


    This example creates a new virtual machine named new 1 that has 512 MB of memory.
    Example 2

    PS C:\> New-VM -Name "new 2" -MemoryStartupBytes 1GB -NewVHDPath d:\vhd\base.vhdx


    This example creates a virtual machine named new 2 that has 1 GB of memory and that is connected to a new 40 GB
    virtual hard disk that uses the VHDX format.
    Example 3

    PS C:\> New-VM -Name "new 3" -MemoryStartupBytes 1GB -VHDPath d:\vhd\BaseImage.vhdx


    This example creates a virtual machine named new 3 that has 1 GB of memory and connects it to an existing virtual
    hard disk that uses the VHDX format.
```

Creating a virtual machine with the New-VM cmdlet comes into play when you need to create a large number of virtual machines with similar specifications. With the simple PowerShell magic of the for-each loop, you can create hundreds of virtual machines with a single cmdlet that use a differencing disk. You can also start the virtual machine when it gets created:

```
1..100 | % {


New-VHD -ParentPath c:\Base.vhdx -Path c:\Diff_VM_$_.vhdx -Differencing;

New-VM -Name vm$_ -MemoryStartupBytes 2GB -VHDPath c:\Diff_VM_$_.vhdx;

Start-VM vm$_


}
```

Deleting a virtual machine

Deleting a virtual machine is relatively simple with PowerShell. Using the Remove-VM PowerShell cmdlet, just type the cmdlet in your PowerShell window to delete the two virtual machines we created in the previous example.

The following example gets the details of all the nodes of the Hyper-V cluster. Next, we use the Remove-VM cmdlet to remove virtual machines with the prefix VMtest followed by the Hyper-V hostname that comes from the pipeline:

```
Get-ClusterNode | select @{l='ComputerName';e={$_.name}} | %
  {Remove-VM -Name VMtest$($_.computername) -ComputerName
  $_.computername }
```

```
PS C:\> Get-ClusterNode | select @{l='ComputerName';e={$_.name}} | % {Remove-VM -Name VMtest$($_.computername) -Computer
Name $_.computername }

Confirm
Are you sure you want to remove virtual machine "VMtesthyperv01"?
[Y] Yes  [A] Yes to All  [N] No  [L] No to All  [S] Suspend  [?] Help (default is "Y"): y

Confirm
Are you sure you want to remove virtual machine "VMtesthyperv02"?
[Y] Yes  [A] Yes to All  [N] No  [L] No to All  [S] Suspend  [?] Help (default is "Y"): y
PS C:\> _
```

You can also delete a set of virtual machines without any user intervention by a single PowerShell cmdlet using the for-each loop. The following command will delete 100 virtual machines that had the prefix VM in front of them:

```
1..100 | % {


Remove-VM -Name vm$_ -Force


}
```

Starting and stopping a virtual machine

Starting and stopping a virtual machine is relatively simple with PowerShell using the Start-VM or Stop-VM PowerShell cmdlet. All you need to do is type the cmdlet in your PowerShell window.

In the following example, we will get the details of all the virtual machines on each of the Hyper-V hosts that are a part of the Hyper-V cluster, and start them:

```
Get-ClusterNode | select @{l='ComputerName';e={$_.name}} | % {Get-VM
  -ComputerName $_.computername | Start-VM}
```

The following screenshot illustrates the output of the preceding command:

```
PS C:\> Get-ClusterNode | select @{l='ComputerName';e={$_.name}} | % {Get-VM -ComputerName $_.computername | Start-VM}

Starting
   10%
     [oooooooooo                                                                                    ]
```

We follow a similar exercise to stop the virtual machines. To do this, we just need to replace the Start-VM cmdlet with Stop-VM. As you can see in the following command, once we issue the cmdlet, it confirms the action and stops / shuts down the VM:

```
Get-ClusterNode | select @{l='ComputerName';e={$_.name}} | %
  {Get-VM -ComputerName $_.computername | Stop-VM}
```

The output is displayed in the following screenshot:

```
PS C:\> Get-ClusterNode | select @{l='ComputerName';e={$_.name}} | % {Get-VM -ComputerName $_.computername | Stop-VM}

Confirm
Hyper-V cannot shut down virtual machine VM11 because the Shutdown integration service is unavailable. To avoid
potential data loss, you can pause or save the state of the virtual machine. The other option is to turn off the
virtual machine, but data loss might occur.
[Y] Yes  [N] No  [S] Suspend  [?] Help (default is "Y"): y

Confirm
Hyper-V cannot shut down virtual machine VM12 because the Shutdown integration service is unavailable. To avoid
potential data loss, you can pause or save the state of the virtual machine. The other option is to turn off the
virtual machine, but data loss might occur.
[Y] Yes  [N] No  [S] Suspend  [?] Help (default is "Y"): y

Confirm
Hyper-V cannot shut down virtual machine VM13 because the Shutdown integration service is unavailable. To avoid
potential data loss, you can pause or save the state of the virtual machine. The other option is to turn off the
virtual machine, but data loss might occur.
[Y] Yes  [N] No  [S] Suspend  [?] Help (default is "Y"): y

Confirm
Hyper-V cannot shut down virtual machine VM14 because the Shutdown integration service is unavailable. To avoid
potential data loss, you can pause or save the state of the virtual machine. The other option is to turn off the
virtual machine, but data loss might occur.
[Y] Yes  [N] No  [S] Suspend  [?] Help (default is "Y"): y

Confirm
Hyper-V cannot shut down virtual machine VM17 because the Shutdown integration service is unavailable. To avoid
potential data loss, you can pause or save the state of the virtual machine. The other option is to turn off the
virtual machine, but data loss might occur.
[Y] Yes  [N] No  [S] Suspend  [?] Help (default is "Y"):
```

Configuring properties on virtual machines

Configuring properties on virtual machines can be done using PowerShell cmdlets that have the Set verb in them. To get a list of all the PowerShell cmdlets that can be used to set a virtual machine's properties, type command shown in the following screenshot, in the PowerShell prompt:

```
PS C:\Users\Administrator> gcm Set-VM*

CommandType      Name                                          ModuleName
-----------      ----                                          ----------
Cmdlet           Set-VM                                        Hyper-V
Cmdlet           Set-VMBios                                    Hyper-V
Cmdlet           Set-VMComPort                                 Hyper-V
Cmdlet           Set-VMDvdDrive                                Hyper-V
Cmdlet           Set-VMFibreChannelHba                         Hyper-V
Cmdlet           Set-VMFirmware                                Hyper-V
Cmdlet           Set-VMFloppyDiskDrive                         Hyper-V
Cmdlet           Set-VMHardDiskDrive                           Hyper-V
Cmdlet           Set-VMHost                                    Hyper-V
Cmdlet           Set-VMMemory                                  Hyper-V
Cmdlet           Set-VMMigrationNetwork                        Hyper-V
Cmdlet           Set-VMNetworkAdapter                          Hyper-V
Cmdlet           Set-VMNetworkAdapterFailoverConfiguration     Hyper-V
Cmdlet           Set-VmNetworkAdapterIsolation                 Hyper-V
Cmdlet           Set-VmNetworkAdapterRoutingDomainMapping      Hyper-V
Cmdlet           Set-VMNetworkAdapterVlan                      Hyper-V
Cmdlet           Set-VMProcessor                               Hyper-V
Cmdlet           Set-VMRemoteFx3dVideoAdapter                  Hyper-V
Cmdlet           Set-VMReplication                             Hyper-V
Cmdlet           Set-VMReplicationAuthorizationEntry           Hyper-V
Cmdlet           Set-VMReplicationServer                       Hyper-V
Cmdlet           Set-VMResourcePool                            Hyper-V
Cmdlet           Set-VMSan                                     Hyper-V
Cmdlet           Set-VMSwitch                                  Hyper-V
Cmdlet           Set-VMSwitchExtensionPortFeature              Hyper-V
Cmdlet           Set-VMSwitchExtensionSwitchFeature            Hyper-V
```

As you can see in the preceding screenshot, there are a number of properties that can be set for the virtual machine, including the BIOS, DVD drive, virtual machine memory, and also network adapter properties. Also, there is a Set-VMHost cmdlet that allows you to set some of the properties related to the Hyper-V host. Let's go through these cmdlets one by one.

Type the following cmdlet in the PowerShell prompt to change the automatic stop action of all the VMs running on both nodes of the Hyper-V cluster:

```
Get-ClusterNode | select @{l='ComputerName';e={$_.name}} | %
  {Get-VM -ComputerName $_.computername |
  Set-VM -AutomaticStopAction shutdown }
```

> The VMs need to be in the shutdown state to change `AutomaticStopAction`.

The following screenshot shows this command:

```
PS C:\> Get-ClusterNode | select @{l='ComputerName';e={$_.name}} | % {Get-VM -ComputerName $_.computername | Set-VM -Aut
omaticStopAction shutdown }
```

The command shown in the preceding screenshot sets the automatic stop action on all the virtual machines to shutdown.

Next, let's change the virtual machine's start up order for all the virtual machines running on both nodes of the Hyper-V cluster by typing the following cmdlet in a PowerShell prompt:

```
Get-ClusterNode | select @{l='ComputerName';e={$_.name}} | %
  {Get-VM -ComputerName $_.computername | Set-VMBios -
  StartupOrder @("Floppy", "LegacyNetworkAdapter", "CD", "IDE")}
```

The following screenshot displays this command:

```
PS C:\> Get-ClusterNode | select @{l='ComputerName';e={$_.name}} | % {Get-VM -ComputerName $_.computername | Set-VMBios
-StartupOrder @("Floppy", "LegacyNetworkAdapter", "CD", "IDE")}
```

The command shown in the preceding screenshot sets the virtual machine's startup order to an order that starts from a floppy to a legacy network adapter to CD and then IDE. For generation 2 virtual machines, you will need to use the `Get-VMFirmware` and `Set-VMFirmware` cmdlets instead. The following example shows how you can use the `Get-VMFirmware` cmdlet to extract firmware details of a generation 2 VM:

```
Get-VMFirmware testvm
```

```
PS C:\> Get-VMFirmware testvm

VMName SecureBoot PreferredNetworkBootProtocol BootOrder
------ ---------- ---------------------------- ---------
testvm On         IPv4                         {Network, Drive}
```

Similarly, you can change firmware properties of a virtual machine using the Set-VMFirmware cmdlet. The following cmdlet allows you to set the Secure Boot property on the VM:

```
Set-VMFirmware "testvm" -EnableSecureBoot Off
```

```
PS C:\> Set-VMFirmware "testvm" -EnableSecureBoot Off
PS C:\> _
```

Now, if we perform a Get-VMFirmware test, we will see that the SecureBoot option for the VM has been disabled:

```
PS C:\> Get-VMFirmware testvm

VMName SecureBoot PreferredNetworkBootProtocol BootOrder
------ ---------- ---------------------------- ---------
testvm Off        IPv4                         {Network, Drive}
```

Next, let's see how we can make configuration changes to virtual processors in a virtual machine. For the following cmdlet example to work, the virtual machines should be in the stopped state:

```
Get-ClusterNode | select @{l='ComputerName';e={$_.name}} | %
  {Get-VM -ComputerName $_.computername | Set-VMProcessor -Count 2
  -Reserve 10 -Maximum 75 -RelativeWeight 200}
```

```
PS C:\> Get-ClusterNode | select @{l='ComputerName';e={$_.name}} | % {Get-VM -ComputerName $_.computername | Set-VMProce
ssor -Count 2 -Reserve 10 -Maximum 75 -RelativeWeight 200}
PS C:\> _
```

The command shown in the preceding screenshot configures all the virtual machines with two virtual processors, a reserve of 10 percent, a limit of 75 percent, and a relative weight of 200. The reserve property specifies the percentage of processor resources to be reserved for a particular virtual machine (allowed values range from 0 to 100). The maximum parameter specifies the maximum percentage of resources available to the virtual machine processor to be configured (allowed values range from 0 to 100). The relative weight specifies the priority for allocating the physical machine's processing power to a virtual machine that is relative to others (allowed values range from 1 to 10,000).

Next, let's see how you can play around with names pipes using the `Set-VMComPort` cmdlet. The following cmdlet, when executed, sets the second VM's COM port on all the virtual machines to a defined value:

```
Get-ClusterNode | select @{l='ComputerName';e={$_.name}} | %
  {Get-VM -ComputerName $_.computername |
  Set-VMComPort Number 2 -Path  "\\.\pipe\TestPipe"}
```

```
PS C:\> Get-ClusterNode | select @{l='ComputerName';e={$_.name}} | % {Get-VM -ComputerName $_.computername | Set-VMComPo
rt 2 "\\.\pipe\TestPipe"}
PS C:\> _
```

The command shown in the preceding screenshot configures the second COM port on all the virtual machines specified by the number 2 to connect to the named pipe `TestPipe` on the local computer. The named pipe option connects the virtual serial port to a Windows-named pipe on the host operating system or a computer on the network.

Next, let's see how you can configure virtual machines to use an ISO file:

```
Get-ClusterNode | select @{l='ComputerName';e={$_.name}} | %
  {Get-VM -ComputerName $_.computername | Get-VMDvdDrive |
  Set-VMDvdDrive -path "\\smb3share\vol_Vinith_Infra\
  en_sql_server_2012_enterprise_edition_x86_x64_dvd_813294.iso"}
```

```
PS C:\> Get-ClusterNode | select @{l='ComputerName';e={$_.name}} | % {Get-VM -ComputerName $_.computername | Get-VMDvdDr
ive | Set-VMDvdDrive -path "\\smb3share\vol_Vinith_Infra\en_sql_server_2012_enterprise_edition_x86_x64_dvd_813294.iso"}
PS C:\>
PS C:\> _
```

The command shown in the preceding screenshot configures the virtual DVD drives of all the virtual machines to use the SQL 2012 installation ISO as its media.

The command, shown in the following screenshot, retrieves the Fibre Channel host bus adapter on a virtual machine and sets the world wide names property in them:

```
PS C:\>Get-VMFibreChannelHba -VMName MyVM | Set-VMFibreChannelHba -GenerateWwn
```

Next, let's configure a virtual machine's HBA adapters using PowerShell:

```
Get-ClusterNode | select @{l='ComputerName';e={$_.name}} | %
  {Get-VM -ComputerName $_.computername | Get-VMFibreChannelHba |
  Set-VMFibreChannelHba -GenerateWwn}
```

```
PS C:\> Get-ClusterNode | select @{l='ComputerName';e={$_.name}} | % {Get-VM -ComputerName $_.computername | Get-VMFibre
ChannelHba | Set-VMFibreChannelHba -GenerateWwn}
PS C:\> _
```

The command shown in the preceding screenshot configures a Fibre Channel host bus adapter to be generated automatically on all virtual machines with world-wide names.

Next, let's have a look at an example of how you can enable Secure Boot on a VM. Note that this option can be configured only on generation 2 virtual machines. In the following example, we will configure Secure Boot on all virtual machines in our Hyper-V cluster, assuming that they all belong to generation 2:

```
PS C:\> Get-ClusterNode | select @{l='ComputerName';e={$_.name}} | % {Get-VM -ComputerName $_.computername | Get-VMFirm
ware | Set-VMFirmware -EnableSecureBoot On}
PS C:\>
PS C:\> _
```

The example shown in the preceding screenshot enables secure boot functionality on the virtual machine on your Hyper-V cluster.

Next, let's look at an example to configure a virtual machine to use a **virtual floppy drive (VFD)**. We will use the logic illustrated in the previous example to set a floppy drive on a set of virtual machines. A VFD is used by some applications in legacy virtual machines.

[Generation 2 virtual machines do not support floppy drives.]

```
PS C:\> Get-ClusterNode | select @{l='ComputerName';e={$_.name}} | % {Get-VM -ComputerName $_.computername | Set-VMFlopp
yDiskDrive -Path c:\test.vfd}
PS C:\> _
```

The command shown in the preceding screenshot connects C:\Test.vfd to the virtual floppy disk of the virtual machine testvm. Next, let's look at an example that shows how we can configure a virtual machine to use a VHD. The following example moves the VHD on all the virtual machines from IDE 1.0 to IDE 1.1.

The following screenshot assumes that you have a hard disk on the 1.0 controller:

```
PS C:\> Get-ClusterNode | select @{l='ComputerName';e={$_.name}} | % {Get-VM -ComputerName $_.computername | Get-VMHard
DiskDrive -ControllerType IDE -ControllerNumber 1 -ControllerLocation 0 | Set-VMHardDiskDrive -ToControllerLocation 1}
PS C:\> _
```

The examples we covered in this section dealt with Hyper-V VMs. Now, let's look at examples to configure properties on the Hyper-V host itself. We will configure our Hyper-V host to allow maximum number of live and storage migrations. The following example sets all the Hyper-V hosts that are part of the Hyper-V cluster to allow 10 simultaneous live and storage migrations:

```
Get-ClusterNode | select @{l='ComputerName';e={$_.name}} | %
  {Set-VMHost -MaximumVirtualMachineMigrations 10 -
  MaximumStorageMigrations 10}
```

```
PS C:\> Get-ClusterNode | select @{l='ComputerName';e={$_.name}} | % {Set-VMHost -MaximumVirtualMachineMigrations 10 -Ma
ximumStorageMigrations 10}
PS C:\> _
```

You can verify that the configuration change for 10 live and storage migrations is successfully set by accessing the Hyper-V settings via the Hyper-V manager's GUI console:

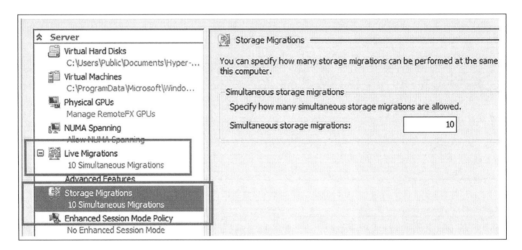

You can also extract this information from a cmdlet, shown as follows:

```
Get-ClusterNode | select @{l='ComputerName';e={$_.name}} | %
  {Get-VMHost} | select ComputerName, MaximumStorageMigrations,
  MaximumVirtualMachineMigrations
```

Next, let's configure the remote video adapter on VMs:

```
PS C:\> Get-ClusterNode | select @{l='ComputerName';e={$_.name}} | % {Get-VM -ComputerName $_.computername | Set-VMRemo
teFx3dVideoAdapter -MaximumResolution 1920x1200}
PS C:\> _
```

The example shown in the preceding screenshot sets the maximum resolution of the RemoteFX adapter on all virtual machines to 1920 x 1200. Note that the RemoteFx Video adapter should be added to the virtual machine for this cmdlet to work:

```
PS C:\> Get-VMSan | Set-VMSan -WorldWideNodeName C003FF0000FFFF22 -WorldWidePortName C003FF5778E50024
```

The example shown in the preceding screenshot configures the entire virtual **storage area network (SAN)** with the specified `WorldWideNodeName` and `WorldWidePortName` values.

Managing VHDs on virtual machines

To get a list of cmdlets that can be used to manage VHDs, type the following command in your PowerShell window:

```
Get-Command *vhd*
```

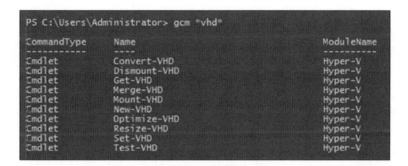

Let's go through some of these cmdlets, shown in the following screenshot, to manage a virtual hard disk. Hyper-V allows you to convert the format, version type, and block size of a VHD file.

The `Convert-VHD` cmdlet allows you to do this. Type the following cmdlet to convert all the virtual hard disks at a specified location from type `.vhdx` to `.vhd`.

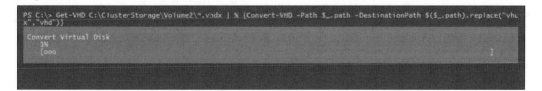

The following example converts a set of disks present at a location, from the source disk of the .VHDX format to a destination-fixed disk of the .VHD format; VHDtype specifies the type of converted VHD:

```
PS C:\> Get-VHD C:\ClusterStorage\Volume2\*.vhdx | % {Convert-VHD -Path $_.path -DestinationPath $($_.path).replace("vhd
x","vhd") -VHDType fixed }
Convert Virtual Disk
   4%
   [oooo                                                                                          ]
```

[Allowed values for the parameter, VHDtype, are Fixed, Dynamic, and Differencing. The default type is determined by the type of source VHD.]

The Dismount-VHD or Mount-VHD cmdlet allows you to dismount or mount an attached VHD. Type the cmdlet shown in the following screenshot to mount and dismount a set of VHDs present at a user-specified location:

```
PS C:\> Get-VHD C:\ClusterStorage\Volume2\*.vhdx | % {Dismount-VHD $_.path}
PS C:\>
```

The command shown in the preceding screenshot dismounts an attached VHD where the path to the VHD file path is c:\clustrstorage\volume2\testvhdx.vhdx:

```
PS C:\> Get-VHD C:\ClusterStorage\Volume2\*.vhdx | % {Mount-VHD $_.path}
PS C:\>
```

The example shown in the preceding screenshot mounts a VHD where the path to the VHD file is C:\ClusterStorage\Volume2\testvhdx.vhdx:

```
PS C:\> Get-VHD C:\ClusterStorage\Volume2\*.vhdx | % {Convert-VHD -Path $_.path -DestinationPath $($_.path).replace("vhd
x","vhd") -VHDType fixed }
Convert Virtual Disk
   4%
   [oooo                                                                                          ]
```

The example shown in the preceding screenshot mounts a set of VHDs present at a location in the read-only mode.

```
Get-VHD C:\ClusterStorage\Volume2\*.vhdx | % {Mount-VHD –Path $_.path
  –PassThru | Get-Disk | Get-Partition | Get-Volume}
```

```
PS C:\> Get-VHD C:\ClusterStorage\Volume2\*.vhdx | % {Mount-VHD –Path $_.path –PassThru | Get-Disk | Get-Partition | Get
-Volume}

DriveLetter     FileSystemLabel  FileSystem   DriveType    HealthStatus    SizeRemaining              Size
-----------     ---------------  ----------   ---------    ------------    -------------              ----
F               System Reserved  NTFS         Fixed        Healthy             89.13 MB             350 MB
G                                NTFS         Fixed        Healthy             91.46 GB           99.66 GB


PS C:\>
```

The example shown in the preceding screenshot attaches a set VHD to the system from a predefined location and gets the volumes associated with it.

```
Get-VHD C:\ClusterStorage\Volume2\*.vhdx
```

```
PS C:\> Get-VHD C:\ClusterStorage\Volume2\*.vhdx

ComputerName            : HYPERV01
Path                    : C:\ClusterStorage\Volume2\VM1.vhdx
VhdFormat               : VHDX
VhdType                 : Dynamic
FileSize                : 8694792192
Size                    : 107374182400
MinimumSize             : 107374182400
LogicalSectorSize       : 512
PhysicalSectorSize      : 4096
BlockSize               : 33554432
ParentPath              :
DiskIdentifier          : 6fcaf23c-e62a-49c3-906d-57241377728f
FragmentationPercentage : 12
Alignment               : 1
Attached                : False
DiskNumber              :
Key                     :
IsDeleted               : False
Number                  :

ComputerName            : HYPERV01
Path                    : C:\ClusterStorage\Volume2\VM10.vhdx
VhdFormat               : VHDX
VhdType                 : Dynamic
FileSize                : 8694792192
Size                    : 107374182400
MinimumSize             : 107374182400
LogicalSectorSize       : 512
PhysicalSectorSize      : 4096
BlockSize               : 33554432
ParentPath              :
DiskIdentifier          : 6fcaf23c-e62a-49c3-906d-57241377728f
FragmentationPercentage : 12
Alignment               : 1
Attached                : False
DiskNumber              :
Key                     :
IsDeleted               : False
Number                  :
```

The command shown in the preceding screenshot gets the details of VHDs that are stored at a predefined location.

```
Get-VHD C:\ClusterStorage\Volume2\*.vhdx | % {Mount-VHD –Path $_.path –
PassThru | Get-Disk}
```

```
PS C:\> Get-VHD C:\ClusterStorage\Volume2\*.vhdx | % {Mount-VHD –Path $_.path -PassThru | Get-Disk}

Number Friendly Name                OperationalStatus              Total Size Partition Style
------ -------------                -----------------              ---------- ---------------
5      Microsoft Virtual Disk       Online                         100 GB MBR
6      Microsoft Virtual Disk       Offline                        100 GB MBR
7      Microsoft Virtual Disk       Offline                        100 GB MBR
8      Microsoft Virtual Disk       Offline                        100 GB MBR
9      Microsoft Virtual Disk       Offline                        100 GB MBR
10     Microsoft Virtual Disk       Offline                        100 GB MBR
11     Microsoft Virtual Disk       Offline                        100 GB MBR
12     Microsoft Virtual Disk       Offline                        100 GB MBR
13     Microsoft Virtual Disk       Offline                        100 GB MBR
14     Microsoft Virtual Disk       Offline                        100 GB MBR
15     Microsoft Virtual Disk       Offline                        100 GB MBR
16     Microsoft Virtual Disk       Offline                        100 GB MBR
17     Microsoft Virtual Disk       Offline                        100 GB MBR
```

The example shown in the preceding screenshot gets the VHD details attached to the system with the associated disk numbers.

```
Get-ClusterNode | select @{l='ComputerName';e={$_.name}} | %
  {Get-VM -ComputerName $_.computername | Select-Object vmid |
  Get-VHD | ft} .
```

```
PS C:\> Get-ClusterNode | select @{l='ComputerName';e={$_.name}} | % {Get-VM -ComputerName $_.computername | Select-Obj
ct vmid | Get-VHD | ft}

ComputerNam Path      VhdFormat  VhdType   FileSize       Size MinimumSize LogicalSect PhysicalSec  BlockSize
e                                                                             orSize       torSize
----------- ----      ---------  -------   --------       ---- ----------- ----------- -----------  ---------
HYPERV01    C:\Clust...   VHDX   Dynamic   8694792192 ...74182400 ...74182400    512        4096     33554432
HYPERV01    C:\Clust...   VHDX   Dynamic   8493465600 ...74182400 ...74182400    512        4096     33554432
HYPERV01    \\10.238...   VHDX   Dynamic   8459911168 ...74182400 ...74182400    512        4096     33554432
HYPERV01    \\10.238...   VHDX   Dynamic   8459911168 ...74182400 ...74182400    512        4096     33554432
HYPERV01    \\10.238...   VHDX   Dynamic   8459911168 ...74182400 ...74182400    512        4096     33554432
HYPERV01    \\10.238...   VHDX   Dynamic   8459911168 ...74182400 ...74182400    512        4096     33554432
HYPERV01    \\10.238...   VHDX   Dynamic   8493465600 ...74182400 ...74182400    512        4096     33554432
HYPERV01    \\10.238...   VHDX   Dynamic   8459911168 ...74182400 ...74182400    512        4096     33554432
HYPERV01    \\10.238...   VHDX   Dynamic   8459911168 ...74182400 ...74182400    512        4096     33554432
HYPERV01    C:\Clust...   VHDX   Dynamic   8493465600 ...74182400 ...74182400    512        4096     33554432
HYPERV01    \\10.238...   VHDX   Dynamic   8459911168 ...74182400 ...74182400    512        4096     33554432
HYPERV01    \\virtua...   VHDX   Dynamic   8493465600 ...74182400 ...74182400    512        4096     33554432
HYPERV01    C:\Clust...   VHDX   Dynamic   8493465600 ...74182400 ...74182400    512        4096     33554432
HYPERV01    C:\Clust...   VHDX   Dynamic   8493465600 ...74182400 ...74182400    512        4096     33554432
HYPERV01    C:\Clust...   VHDX   Dynamic   8493465600 ...74182400 ...74182400    512        4096     33554432
```

The example shown in the preceding screenshot gets the VHD objects associated with all the virtual machines that are a part of the Hyper-V cluster using the pipeline feature for the Path parameter.

```
Merge-VHD C:\ClusterStorage\Volume1\VM4\VM4_
  48706D46-8C3C-414B-B535-DA905237BE81.avhdx
```

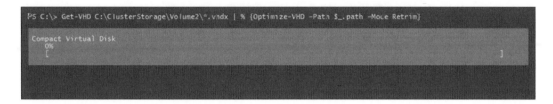

The example shown in the preceding screenshot merges the avhdx file present at a location to its parent VHD. The Merge-VHD cmdlet merges VHDs in a differencing VHD chain. The merge happens from a specified source-child disk to a specified destination child disk. Merge is an offline operation; the VHD chain must not be attached when this is initiated.

The example shown in the preceding screenshot runs the compact operation in the Retrim mode on a set of VHDs present at a location.

[Before executing the next cmdlet, make sure that the drive is dismounted/offline or is in the read-only mode.]

```
Optimize-VHD -Path c:\test\dynamic.vhdx -Mode Quick
```

The example shown in the preceding screenshot runs the compact operation in the Quick mode on a set of VHDs.

The example shown in the preceding screenshot shrinks the VHDX files present at a location to a size of 150 GB (assuming that the VHD object associated with the file path has a minimum size less than or equal to 150 GB).

 Before executing the next cmdlet, make sure that the drive is dismounted / offline or is in the read-only mode.

```
Get-VHD C:\ClusterStorage\Volume2\*.vhdx | %
  {Resize-VHD -Path $_.path -ToMinimumSize}
```

```
PS C:\> Get-VHD C:\ClusterStorage\Volume2\*.vhdx | % {Resize-VHD -Path $_.path -ToMinimumSize}

Resize Virtual Disk
       0%
       [                                                                        ]
```

The example shown in the preceding screenshot shrinks the VHDX files present at a predefined location to its minimum possible size.

```
PS C:\> Get-VHD C:\ClusterStorage\Volume2\*.vhdx | % {Set-VHD -Path $_.path -PhysicalSectorSizeBytes 512}
PS C:\>
```

This example shown in the preceding screenshot sets the physical sector size of all the VHDX files present at a location to 512 bytes.

```
Get-VHD C:\ClusterStorage\Volume2\*.vhdx | % {Test-VHD -Path $_.path}
```

```
PS C:\> Get-VHD C:\ClusterStorage\Volume2\*.vhdx | % {Test-VHD -Path $_.path}
True
True
True
True
True
True
True
True
True
True
True
True
True
PS C:\>
```

The example shown in the preceding screenshot tests whether the VHD chain at a location is in a usable state.

Summary

In this chapter, we covered important cmdlets related to configuring and extracting properties about virtual machines and their associated Hyper-V hosts. In the next chapter, we will cover the other set of relevant cmdlets that can be used to automate Hyper-V administrative tasks in detail.

3
Managing Your Hyper-V Virtual Machines

In this chapter, we will continue to explore the PowerShell cmdlets available in the Hyper-V PowerShell module to manage virtual machine infrastructure components. This chapter has been subdivided into smaller sections and we will be covering the following topics:

- Managing virtual switches and virtual network adapters in virtual machines
- Managing virtual machine migrations
- Managing virtual machine imports, exports, and snapshots
- Managing virtual machine backups with Hyper-V Replica
- Managing virtual machine connect

We will start by taking a deep dive into cmdlets, which can help us manage the virtual machine switches and network adapters; this will help us to understand the various ways to automate network configuration for virtual machines. Next, we will explore the cmdlets that allow a Hyper-V admin to manage virtual machine migrations across hosts and clusters. After that, we will explore cmdlets that allow us to export, import, and use snapshot-based technology on virtual machines, which aids in the quick testing of installed applications on virtual machines and also serves as a backup mechanism. Next, we will also explore the cmdlets related to Hyper-V Replica—a new disaster recovery technology—which allows an administrator to back up a virtual machine to a secondary site and maintain its high availability when the primary data center goes offline. Lastly, we will explore virtual machine connect—a new feature that uses the VMBus as a connection path and allows the administrator to connect to virtual machines without using a network connection.

Managing virtual switches and virtual network adapters

The Hyper-V PowerShell module comes with a set of cmdlets, which can be used to manage the virtual machine network adapters and virtual switches. Virtual machine networks and switches form the core networking component of virtual machines. Virtual switch is a software-based network switch that helps in connecting virtual machines to virtual and physical networks. They can be of three types: external, internal, and private. Once the virtual switches are created, the virtual network adapters created for a virtual machine can be tagged to these virtual switches, allowing the virtual machine to connect to both physical and virtual networks. The virtual network adapters assigned to a virtual machine require it to have the required drivers provided by integration services to be installed on it.

Open a PowerShell prompt, and type the cmdlets shown in the following screenshot to get a list of all the cmdlets that are available to manage the virtual network and virtual switches:

```
PS C:\Users\Administrator> gcm *network* -Module hyper-v

CommandType     Name                                          ModuleName
-----------     ----                                          ----------
Cmdlet          Add-VMMigrationNetwork                        Hyper-V
Cmdlet          Add-VMNetworkAdapter                          Hyper-V
Cmdlet          Add-VMNetworkAdapterAcl                       Hyper-V
Cmdlet          Add-VMNetworkAdapterExtendedAcl               Hyper-V
Cmdlet          Add-VmNetworkAdapterRoutingDomainMapping      Hyper-V
Cmdlet          Connect-VMNetworkAdapter                      Hyper-V
Cmdlet          Disconnect-VMNetworkAdapter                   Hyper-V
Cmdlet          Get-VMMigrationNetwork                        Hyper-V
Cmdlet          Get-VMNetworkAdapter                          Hyper-V
Cmdlet          Get-VMNetworkAdapterAcl                       Hyper-V
Cmdlet          Get-VMNetworkAdapterExtendedAcl               Hyper-V
Cmdlet          Get-VMNetworkAdapterFailoverConfiguration     Hyper-V
Cmdlet          Get-VmNetworkAdapterIsolation                 Hyper-V
Cmdlet          Get-VMNetworkAdapterRoutingDomainMapping      Hyper-V
Cmdlet          Get-VMNetworkAdapterVlan                      Hyper-V
Cmdlet          Remove-VMMigrationNetwork                     Hyper-V
Cmdlet          Remove-VMNetworkAdapter                       Hyper-V
Cmdlet          Remove-VMNetworkAdapterAcl                    Hyper-V
Cmdlet          Remove-VMNetworkAdapterExtendedAcl            Hyper-V
Cmdlet          Remove-VMNetworkAdapterRoutingDomainMapping   Hyper-V
Cmdlet          Rename-VMNetworkAdapter                       Hyper-V
Cmdlet          Set-VMMigrationNetwork                        Hyper-V
Cmdlet          Set-VMNetworkAdapter                          Hyper-V
Cmdlet          Set-VMNetworkAdapterFailoverConfiguration     Hyper-V
Cmdlet          Set-VmNetworkAdapterIsolation                 Hyper-V
Cmdlet          Set-VmNetworkAdapterRoutingDomainMapping      Hyper-V
Cmdlet          Set-VMNetworkAdapterVlan                      Hyper-V
Cmdlet          Test-VMNetworkAdapter                         Hyper-V
```

Let's explore these cmdlets and look at their real-world applications.

Managing a virtual machine's migration networks

Let's look at how to add an IPv4 address range as a possible live migration network on the local Hyper-V host by using a subnet mask:

1. Open a PowerShell prompt and type the command shown in the following screenshot:

```
PS C:\>Add-VMMigrationNetwork 192.168.10.0/24
```

2. Once we execute the cmdlet shown in the preceding screenshot, we will be able to see that the network has been added as a live migration network in the Hyper-V manager:

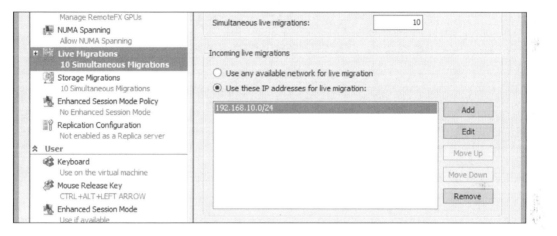

This can also be attained by executing the Get-VMMigrationNetwork cmdlet:

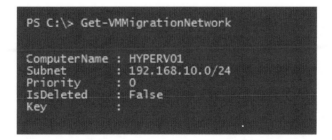

```
PS C:\> Get-VMMigrationNetwork

ComputerName : HYPERV01
Subnet       : 192.168.10.0/24
Priority     : 0
IsDeleted    : False
Key          :
```

3. Similarly, one can use the `Remove-VMMigrationNetwork` cmdlet to remove the virtual machine migration network that has been assigned to the Hyper-V host.

4. The command shown in the following screenshot removes all the networks starting with the address, `192.168`, for the migration:

```
PS C:\>Remove-VMMigrationNetwork 192.168.*
```

5. To get a list of all the virtual machine's live migration networks on the system, type the cmdlet shown in the following screenshot:

```
PS C:\> Get-VMMigrationNetwork

ComputerName : SERVER4
Subnet       : 10.238.187.69/32
Priority     : 5000
IsDeleted    : False
Key          :

ComputerName : SERVER4
Subnet       : fe80::a948:3614:102e:8659%14/128
Priority     : 5000
IsDeleted    : False
Key          :
```

Next, we will look at an example, which adds an **Access Control List (ACL)** to allow the virtual machine, `testvm`, to send and receive from traffic on the IP subnet, `192.168.11.0/24`. Executing this cmdlet creates an ACL that can be applied to specific traffic that is passing through a virtual machine network.

6. You can also use the `Get-NetworkadapterAcl` cmdlet to verify the changes that were made:

```
PS C:\> Add-VMNetworkAdapterAcl -VMName testvm -RemoteIPAddress 192.168.11.0/24 -Direction both -Action Allow
PS C:\> Get-VMNetworkAdapterAcl -VMName testvm

VMName: testvm
VMId: 6a8983e7-605e-423c-b33b-11ba15e81411
AdapterName: Network Adapter
AdapterId: Microsoft:6A8983E7-605E-423C-B33B-11BA15E81411\C56E6337-DC9F-4F50-815D-7FD77CB2F1E9

Direction    Address                                              Action
---------    -------                                              ------
Inbound      Remote 192.168.11.0/24                               Allow
Outbound     Remote 192.168.11.0/24                               Allow

PS C:\> _
```

Configuring virtual machine network adapters with a virtual switch

Now, we will look at the cmdlets that can be used to manage virtual machine migration networks, and later, we will look at some examples on how you can use the Connect and Disconnect network adapter cmdlets to assign a network adapter to a virtual switch.

The InternetAccess cmdlet will connect a virtual network adapter named Internet present in virtual machines Test1 and Test2 to a virtual switch named. For the command shown in the following screenshot to work, the prerequisite is that there should be a network adapter named Internet present on both these virtual machines:

```
PS C:\>Connect-VMNetworkAdapter -VMName Test1,Test2 -Name Internet -SwitchName InternetAccess
```

Another use case would be to connect all the virtual machine network adapters present on a virtual machine to a virtual switch. The next example shows how this can be done by using the PowerShell pipeline. The cmdlet shown in the following screenshot illustrates how you can connect all the virtual network adapters in a virtual machine, Test1, to a virtual switch, InternetAccess:

```
PS C:\>Get-VMNetworkAdapter -VMName Test1 | Connect-VMNetworkAdapter -SwitchName InternetAccess
```

Similarly, let's look at another use case to disconnect all the virtual machine networks from a virtual switch that is available on all the virtual machines hosted on the Hyper-V host. The cmdlet shown in the following screenshot disconnects all the virtual network adapters whose switch name is InternetAccess in all the virtual machines on the local Hyper-V server:

```
PS C:\>Get-VMNetworkAdapter -VMName * | Where-Object {$_.SwitchName -eq 'InternetAccess'} |
Disconnect-VMNetworkAdapter
```

Next, we will take a look at an easy way to extract all the virtual networks attached to the virtual machine. Executing the cmdlet shown in the following screenshot gives more details about the virtual switch MAC addresses and also the IP addresses:

```
PS C:\> Get-VMNetworkAdapter -VMName *

Name               IsManagementOs VMName                        SwitchName           MacAddress    Status IPAddresses
----               -------------- ------                        ----------           ----------    ------ -----------
Network Adapter    False          wfaservernew                  VirtualUplink-Teamed 00155D018865  {Ok}   {10.238.231.44}
Network Adapter    False          WFA_Server                    VirtualUplink-Teamed 00155D01885D  {Ok}   {10.238.188.21}
Network Adapter    False          VirtualCloud_DomainController VirtualUplink-Teamed 00155D018856  {Ok}   {10.238.188.15}
Network Adapter    False          SCVMM2012R2_DrSite            VirtualUplink-Teamed 00155D01885E  {Ok}   {10.238.188.25}
Network Adapter    False          SCVMM2012R2                   VirtualUplink-Teamed 00155D018858  {Ok}   {10.238.188.19}
Network Adapter    False          SCSM2012R2                    VirtualUplink-Teamed 00155D01885A  {Ok}   {10.238.188.18}
Network Adapter    False          scorchscsm2012sp1             VirtualUplink-Teamed 00155D018862  {Ok}   {10.238.231.43}
Network Adapter    False          SCORCH2012R2                  VirtualUplink-Teamed 00155D018859  {Ok}   {10.238.188.17}
Network Adapter    False          SCOM2012R2-OCPM 4.0.1         VirtualUplink-Teamed 00155D01885C          {}
Network Adapter    False          SCOM2012R2                    VirtualUplink-Teamed 00155D018857  {Ok}   {10.238.188.16}
Network Adapter    False          MSBUWFA_DC                    VirtualUplink-Teamed 00155D018866  {Ok}   {10.238.231.45}
Network Adapter    False          exchange3                     VirtualUplink-Teamed 00155D018861  {Ok}   {10.238.231.42}
Network Adapter    False          exchange2                     VirtualUplink-Teamed 00155D018860  {Ok}   {10.238.231.41}
Network Adapter    False          exchange1                     VirtualUplink-Teamed 00155D01885F  {Ok}   {10.238.231.40}
```

The cmdlet shown in the preceding screenshot when run with the −All switch gives details on all the virtual network adapters on both the virtual machines and the management switches:

```
PS C:\> Get-VMNetworkAdapter -All

Name                 IsManagementOs VMName                        SwitchName           MacAddress    Status IPAddresses
----                 -------------- ------                        ----------           ----------    ------ -----------
VirtualUplink-Teamed True                                         VirtualUplink-Teamed 0019999EF827  {Ok}
Network Adapter      False          exchange1                     VirtualUplink-Teamed 00155D01885F  {Ok}   {10.238.2...
Network Adapter      False          exchange2                     VirtualUplink-Teamed 00155D018860  {Ok}   {10.238.2...
Network Adapter      False          exchange3                     VirtualUplink-Teamed 00155D018861  {Ok}   {10.238.2...
Network Adapter      False          MSBUWFA_DC                    VirtualUplink-Teamed 00155D018866  {Ok}   {10.238.2...
Network Adapter      False          SCOM2012R2                    VirtualUplink-Teamed 00155D018857  {Ok}   {10.238.1...
Network Adapter      False          SCOM2012R2-OCPM 4.0.1         VirtualUplink-Teamed 00155D01885C          {}
Network Adapter      False          SCORCH2012R2                  VirtualUplink-Teamed 00155D018859  {Ok}   {10.238.1...
Network Adapter      False          scorchscsm2012sp1             VirtualUplink-Teamed 00155D018862  {Ok}   {10.238.2...
Network Adapter      False          SCSM2012R2                    VirtualUplink-Teamed 00155D01885A  {Ok}   {10.238.1...
Network Adapter      False          SCVMM2012R2                   VirtualUplink-Teamed 00155D018858  {Ok}   {10.238.1...
Network Adapter      False          SCVMM2012R2_DrSite            VirtualUplink-Teamed 00155D01885E  {Ok}   {10.238.1...
Network Adapter      False          VirtualCloud_DomainController VirtualUplink-Teamed 00155D018856  {Ok}   {10.238.1...
Network Adapter      False          WFA_Server                    VirtualUplink-Teamed 00155D01885D  {Ok}   {10.238.1...
Network Adapter      False          wfaservernew                  VirtualUplink-Teamed 00155D018865  {Ok}   {10.238.2...
```

Configuring virtual machine network failover settings

Hyper-V allows an administrator to configure failover capabilities for a virtual machine's network adapter IP address after the Hyper-V Replica recovers the virtual machine at the disaster recovery site; these failover details can be extracted and set up by using the next cmdlet. The cmdlet shown in the following screenshot configures a failover IPv4 address for the virtual network adapter, NetworkAdapter01, on a virtual machine, VM01:

```
PS C:\>Get-VMNetworkAdapter VM01 NetworkAdapter01 | Set-VMNetworkAdapterFailoverConfiguration -IPv4Address
10.100.1.100 -IPv4SubnetMask 255.255.255.0
```

The cmdlet shown in the following screenshot clears the current failover IPv4 settings on the virtual network adapter, NetworkAdapter01, for a virtual machine, VM01:

```
PS C:\>Get-VMNetworkAdapter VM01 NetworkAdapter01 | Set-VMNetworkAdapterFailoverConfiguration
-ClearFailoverIPv4Settings
```

The cmdlet shown in the following screenshot clears the current failover IPv6 settings on a virtual network adapter NetworkAdapter01 for a virtual machine, VM01:

```
PS C:\>Get-VMNetworkAdapter VM01 NetworkAdapter01 | Set-VMNetworkAdapterFailoverConfiguration
-ClearFailoverIPv6Settings
```

The cmdlet shown in the following screenshot obtains the failover IP address configuration of all the virtual network adapters attached to a virtual machine named VM01:

```
PS C:\>Get-VMNetworkAdapterFailoverConfiguration VM01
```

Adding, removing, and renaming virtual machine network adapters

Adding a new virtual machine network adapter to a virtual machine is relatively simple by using the Add-VMNetworkAdapter cmdlet. The cmdlet shown in the following screenshot adds a network adapter, New Network, to a virtual machine named SCOM2012R2_1:

```
PS C:\> Add-VMNetworkAdapter -VMName scom2012r2_1 -VMNetworkAdapterName "New Network"
PS C:\> _
```

You can also remove the virtual machine network adapter attached to a virtual machine by using the `Remove-VMNetworkAdapter` cmdlet. The example shown in the following screenshot removes the network adapter, `Network Adapter`, from a virtual machine named `SCOM2012R2_1`:

```
PS C:\> Remove-VMNetworkAdapter -VMName SCOM2012R2_1  -VMNetworkAdapterName "Network Adapter"
PS C:\> _
```

Similarly, the example shown in the following screenshot renames all the virtual network adapters of a virtual machine, `SCOM2012R2`, to `NewNetwork`:

```
PS C:\> Rename-VMNetworkAdapter -VMName scom2012r2 -NewName NewNetwork_
```

Configuring a virtual machine's network adapter VLANs

Hyper-V PowerShell cmdlets also allow the administrator to assign a VLAN to a virtual machine network. The cmdlet shown in the following screenshot sets the virtual network adapter(s) in the virtual machine, `scom2012r2_1`, to the `Access` mode; also, the traffic sent by this virtual machine is tagged with the VLAN ID, `2`:

```
PS C:\> Set-VMNetworkAdapterVlan -VMName scom2012r2_1 -Access -VlanId 2
PS C:\> _
```

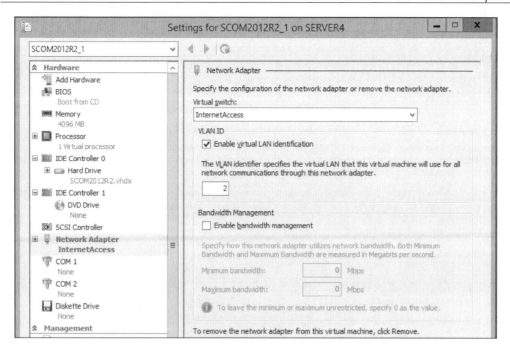

The `Get-VMNetworkAdapterVlan` cmdlet can also be used to extract the preceding information. We can also untag virtual machines from a VLAN. The example shown in the following screenshot gets the virtual machine, `scom2012r2`, and sets the virtual network adapters in the virtual machine to the `Untagged` mode:

Configuring Hyper-V virtual switches and their properties

Now that we have explored the cmdlets for managing virtual network adapters, let's look at the cmdlets to manage and configure Hyper-V virtual switches. The Hyper-V PowerShell module also comes with cmdlets to manage virtual machine switches. To get the list of cmdlets that can be used to manage the virtual switch, type the command shown in the following screenshot in a PowerShell prompt:

```
PS C:\Users\Administrator> gcm *switch* -Module hyper-v

CommandType     Name                                        ModuleName
-----------     ----                                        ----------
Cmdlet          Add-VMSwitch                                Hyper-V
Cmdlet          Add-VMSwitchExtensionPortFeature            Hyper-V
Cmdlet          Add-VMSwitchExtensionSwitchFeature          Hyper-V
Cmdlet          Disable-VMSwitchExtension                   Hyper-V
Cmdlet          Enable-VMSwitchExtension                    Hyper-V
Cmdlet          Get-VMSwitch                                Hyper-V
Cmdlet          Get-VMSwitchExtension                       Hyper-V
Cmdlet          Get-VMSwitchExtensionPortData               Hyper-V
Cmdlet          Get-VMSwitchExtensionPortFeature            Hyper-V
Cmdlet          Get-VMSwitchExtensionSwitchData             Hyper-V
Cmdlet          Get-VMSwitchExtensionSwitchFeature          Hyper-V
Cmdlet          Get-VMSystemSwitchExtension                 Hyper-V
Cmdlet          Get-VMSystemSwitchExtensionPortFeature      Hyper-V
Cmdlet          Get-VMSystemSwitchExtensionSwitchFeature    Hyper-V
Cmdlet          New-VMSwitch                                Hyper-V
Cmdlet          Remove-VMSwitch                             Hyper-V
Cmdlet          Remove-VMSwitchExtensionPortFeature         Hyper-V
Cmdlet          Remove-VMSwitchExtensionSwitchFeature       Hyper-V
Cmdlet          Rename-VMSwitch                             Hyper-V
Cmdlet          Set-VMSwitch                                Hyper-V
Cmdlet          Set-VMSwitchExtensionPortFeature            Hyper-V
Cmdlet          Set-VMSwitchExtensionSwitchFeature          Hyper-V
```

Next, let's look at some of the cmdlets from each of the sections shown in the preceding screenshot. You can add a VM switch to a resource pool using the Add-VMSwitch cmdlet. Grouping the VM switches to resource pools allows them to be managed more easily. The example shown in the following screenshot adds a virtual switch, Test, to the Ethernet resource pool, Engineering Department:

```
PS C:\>Add-VMSwitch -Name Test -ResourcePoolName "Engineering Department"
```

Next, let's look at another example where we assign a virtual machine switch named Test on the Hyper-V host to the Engineering Department resource pool using the PowerShell pipeline. The example shown in the following screenshot adds a virtual switch, Test, to the Ethernet resource pool, Engineering Department:

```
PS C:\>Get-VMSwitch -Name Test | Add-VMSwitch -ResourcePoolName "Engineering Department"
```

Let's see an example of how to work with port security for a virtual machine switch. The example shown in the following screenshot adds a feature to the virtual machine, VM2. The feature here is port security that is supported by the extension — Microsoft Virtual Ethernet Switch Native Extension:

```
PS C:\>$feature = Get-VMSystemSwitchExtensionPortFeature -FeatureName "Ethernet Switch Port Security Settings"
PS C:\>$feature.SettingData.EnableDhcpGuard = $true
PS C:\>$feature.SettingData.EnableRouterGuard = $true
PS C:\>Add-VMSwitchExtensionPortFeature -VMName VM2 -VMSwitchExtensionFeature $feature

Adds a feature to virtual machine VM2. The feature here is a port security feature supported by the extension
Microsoft Virtual Ethernet Switch Native Extension.
```

Let's see an example of how to add some features to a virtual switch. The example shown in the following screenshot illustrates how you can add a feature to the virtual switch, External:

```
PS C:\>$feature = Get-VMSwitchExtensionSwitchFeature -FeatureName "Ethernet Switch BandwidthSettings"
PS C:\>$feature.SettingData.DefaultFlowReservation = 300000000
PS C:\>Add-VMSwitchExtensionSwitchFeature "External" -VMSwitchExtensionSwitchFeature $feature
```

You can also enable and disable a virtual machine switch extension using PowerShell. The next example shows how you can do this. The following example disables the WFP, "Microsoft Windows Filtering Platform", on the virtual switch, Internal Switch:

```
PS C:\>Disable-VMSwitchExtension -VMSwitchName "Internal Switch" -Name "Microsoft Windows Filtering Platform"
```

The example shown in the following screenshot enables the WFP, "Microsoft Windows Filtering Platform", on a virtual switch named External:

```
PS C:\>Enable-VMSwitchExtension -VMSwitchName External -Name "Microsoft Windows Filtering Platform"
```

The example shown in the following screenshot gets virtual switches from one or more virtual Hyper-V hosts:

```
PS C:\> Get-VMSwitch

Name                    SwitchType  NetAdapterInterfaceDescription
----                    ----------  ------------------------------
VirtualUplink-Teamed    External    Intel(R) 82580 Gigabit Network Connection
InternetAccess          Private


PS C:\> _
```

The example shown in the following screenshot gets all the virtual switches that connect to the external network:

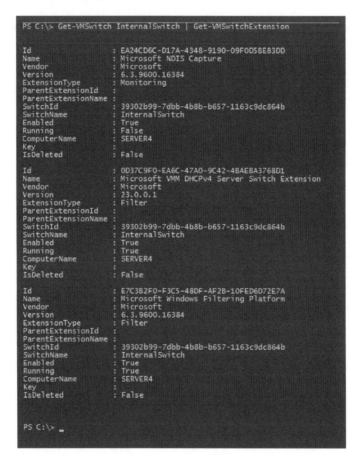

The example shown in the following screenshot gets all the virtual switch extensions available to the virtual switch, `InternalSwitch`:

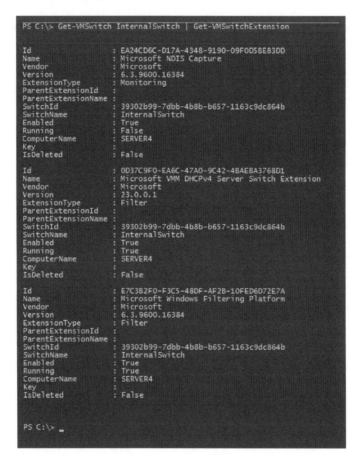

The example shown in the following screenshot gets the port data of the VM switch extension for the virtual machine, scom2012r2:

```
PS C:\> Get-VMSwitchExtensionPortData -VMName scom2012r2

VMId                   : d61e57e3-5ef2-4208-9f5b-a8d8488e6f7e
VMName                 : SCOM2012R2
VMNetworkAdapterName   : NewNetwork
Id                     : ce2fcb7b-b5cd-4eae-b467-94058d7de06e
ExtensionId            : 0D37C9F0-EA6C-47A0-9C42-4BAEBA3768D1
ExtensionName          : Microsoft VMM DHCPv4 Server Switch Extension
Name                   : Microsoft VMM Network Virtualization Port DHCPv4 Information
ComputerName           : SERVER4
Data                   : \\SERVER4\root\virtualization\v2:Msvmm_DhcpV4PortInfo.CreationClassName="Msvmm_DhcpV4PortInfo",D
                         eviceCreationClassName="Msvm_EthernetSwitchPort",DeviceID="48C96A0D-C644-477D-813F-A3AE9AAEFD5A"
                         ,Name="00000000-0000-0000-0000-000000000000",SystemCreationClassName="Msvm_VirtualEthernetSwitch
                         ",SystemName="FA090425-7A12-4E0A-923D-413C0E7D5860"

VMId                   : d61e57e3-5ef2-4208-9f5b-a8d8488e6f7e
VMName                 : SCOM2012R2
VMNetworkAdapterName   : NewNetwork
Id                     : c885bfd1-abb7-418f-8163-9f379c9f7166
ExtensionId            : 11EC6134-128A-4A23-B12F-164184B48348
ExtensionName          : Microsoft Virtual Ethernet Switch Native Extension
Name                   : Ethernet Switch Port Offload Feature Status
ComputerName           : SERVER4
Data                   : \\SERVER4\root\virtualization\v2:Msvm_EthernetSwitchPortOffloadData.CreationClassName="Msvm_Ethe
                         rnetSwitchPortOffloadData",DeviceCreationClassName="Msvm_EthernetSwitchPort",DeviceID="48C96A0D-
                         C644-477D-813F-A3AE9AAEFD5A",Name="00000000-0000-0000-0000-000000000000",SystemCreationClassName
                         ="Msvm_VirtualEthernetSwitch",SystemName="FA090425-7A12-4E0A-923D-413C0E7D5860"

VMId                   : d61e57e3-5ef2-4208-9f5b-a8d8488e6f7e
VMName                 : SCOM2012R2
VMNetworkAdapterName   : NewNetwork
Id                     : 24ad3ce1-69bd-4978-b2ac-daad389d699c
ExtensionId            : 11EC6134-128A-4A23-B12F-164184B48348
ExtensionName          : Microsoft Virtual Ethernet Switch Native Extension
Name                   : Ethernet Switch Port Bandwidth Feature Status
ComputerName           : SERVER4
Data                   : \\SERVER4\root\virtualization\v2:Msvm_EthernetSwitchPortBandwidthData.CreationClassName="Msvm_Et
                         hernetSwitchPortBandwidthData",DeviceCreationClassName="Msvm_EthernetSwitchPort",DeviceID="48C96
                         A0D-C644-477D-813F-A3AE9AAEFD5A",Name="00000000-0000-0000-0000-000000000000",SystemCreationClass
                         Name="Msvm_VirtualEthernetSwitch",SystemName="FA090425-7A12-4E0A-923D-413C0E7D5860"
```

The example shown in the following screenshot gets a feature configured on the virtual machine, scom2012r2, by the Ethernet Switch Port security settings:

```
PS C:\> Get-VMSwitchExtensionPortFeature -VMName scom2012r2 -FeatureName "Ethernet Switch Port Offload Feature Status"
PS C:\>
```

The example shown in the following screenshot gets the switch data from a virtual switch extension that is configured on the virtual switch, External:

```
PS C:\>Get-VMSwitchExtensionSwitchData External -FeatureId 1c37e01c-0cd6-496f-9076-90c131033dc2
```

The example shown in the following screenshot gets all the virtual switch extensions that are installed on the system:

```
PS C:\> Get-VMSystemSwitchExtensionSwitchFeature

Id            : 8b54c928-eb03-4aff-8039-99171dd900ff
ExtensionId   : 11EC6134-128A-4A23-812F-164184B48348
ExtensionName : Microsoft Virtual Ethernet Switch Native Extension
Name          :  SCVMM Ethernet Switch Feature Internal Settings
ComputerName  : SERVER4
SettingData   : \\SERVER4\root\virtualization\v2:Scvmm_VirtualEthernetSwitchInternalSettingData.InstanceID="Microsoft:D
                efinition\\8B54C928-EB03-4AFF-8039-99171DD900FF\\Default"

Id            : 8e540f36-bdf7-47d3-a99a-7055abe2ff4e
ExtensionId   : 11EC6134-128A-4A23-812F-164184B48348
ExtensionName : Microsoft Virtual Ethernet Switch Native Extension
Name          : Virtual Ethernet Switch Network Virtualization Settings
ComputerName  : SERVER4
SettingData   : \\SERVER4\root\virtualization\v2:Scvmm_VirtualEthernetSwitchHyperVNetworkVirtualizationSettingData.Inst
                anceID="Microsoft:Definition\\8E540F36-BDF7-47D3-A99A-7055ABE2FF4E\\Default"

Id            : 3eb2b8e8-4abf-4dbf-9071-16dd47481fbe
ExtensionId   : 11EC6134-128A-4A23-812F-164184B48348
ExtensionName : Microsoft Virtual Ethernet Switch Native Extension
Name          : Ethernet Switch Bandwidth Settings
ComputerName  : SERVER4
SettingData   : \\SERVER4\root\virtualization\v2:Msvm_VirtualEthernetSwitchBandwidthSettingData.InstanceID="Microsoft:D
                efinition\\3EB2B8E8-4ABF-4D8F-9071-16DD47481FBE\\Default"
```

The example shown in the following screenshot gets the features that are configured on a virtual switch:

```
PS C:\> Get-VMSystemSwitchExtension

Id            : 0D37C9F0-EA6C-47A0-9C42-4BAEBA3768D1
Name          : Microsoft VMM DHCPv4 Server Switch Extension
Vendor        : Microsoft
Version       : 23.0.0.1
ExtensionType : Filter
ComputerName  : SERVER4
Key           :
IsDeleted     : False

Id            : E7C3B2F0-F3C5-48DF-AF2B-10FED6D72E7A
Name          : Microsoft Windows Filtering Platform
Vendor        : Microsoft
Version       : 6.3.9600.16384
ExtensionType : Filter
ComputerName  : SERVER4
Key           :
IsDeleted     : False

Id            : EA24CD6C-D17A-4348-9190-09F0D5BE83DD
Name          : Microsoft NDIS Capture
Vendor        : Microsoft
Version       : 6.3.9600.16384
ExtensionType : Monitoring
ComputerName  : SERVER4
Key           :
IsDeleted     : False

Id            : 11EC6134-128A-4A23-812F-164184B48348
Name          : Microsoft Virtual Ethernet Switch Native Extension
Vendor        : Microsoft
Version       : 6.3.9600.16384
ExtensionType : Native
ComputerName  : SERVER4
Key           :
IsDeleted     : False


PS C:\> _
```

The example shown in the following screenshot gets all port-level features, supported by various virtual switch extensions, which are installed on the system and can be configured on a virtual network adapter on Hyper-V:

```
PS C:\> Get-VMSystemSwitchExtensionPortFeature

Id            : f0f00d9f-f2a1-4a0e-bf0a-4c5791db124a
ExtensionId   : 0D37C9F0-EA6C-47A0-9C42-4BAEBA3768D1
ExtensionName : Microsoft VMM DHCPv4 Server Switch Extension
Name          : Microsoft VMM Network Virtualization Port DHCPv4 Binding Options Policy
ComputerName  : SERVER4
SettingData   : \\SERVER4\root\virtualization\v2:Msvmm_DhcpV4PortBindingOptionsPolicy.InstanceID="Microsoft:Definition\
                \F0F00D9F-F2A1-4A0E-BF0A-4C5791DB124A\\Default"

Id            : 085e0abf-cf4c-423c-97b5-857e74dfa1af
ExtensionId   : 0D37C9F0-EA6C-47A0-9C42-4BAEBA3768D1
ExtensionName : Microsoft VMM DHCPv4 Server Switch Extension
Name          : Microsoft VMM Network Virtualization Port DHCPv4 Reservation Policy
ComputerName  : SERVER4
SettingData   : \\SERVER4\root\virtualization\v2:Msvmm_DhcpV4PortReservationPolicy.InstanceID="Microsoft:Definition\\08
                5E0ABF-CF4C-423C-97B5-857E74DFA1AF\\Default"

Id            : 2c0a8f5d-4238-47fe-b96b-da3e6cf136da
ExtensionId   : 0D37C9F0-EA6C-47A0-9C42-4BAEBA3768D1
ExtensionName : Microsoft VMM DHCPv4 Server Switch Extension
Name          : Microsoft VMM Network Virtualization Port Policy
ComputerName  : SERVER4
SettingData   : \\SERVER4\root\virtualization\v2:Msvmm_DhcpV4PortPolicy.InstanceID="Microsoft:Definition\\2C0A8F5D-4238
                -47FE-B96B-DA3E6CF136DA\\Default"

Id            : 83af2ccb-72c9-4479-a285-94e58a98caa6
ExtensionId   : 11EC6134-128A-4A23-B12F-164184B48348
ExtensionName : Microsoft Virtual Ethernet Switch Native Extension
Name          : Ethernet Switch Port Isolation Settings
ComputerName  : SERVER4
SettingData   : \\SERVER4\root\virtualization\v2:Msvm_EthernetSwitchPortIsolationSettingData.InstanceID="Microsoft:Defi
                nition\\83AF2CCB-72C9-4479-A285-94E58A98CAA6\\Default"

Id            : 952c5004-4465-451c-8cb8-fa9ab382b773
ExtensionId   : 11EC6134-128A-4A23-B12F-164184B48348
ExtensionName : Microsoft Virtual Ethernet Switch Native Extension
Name          : Ethernet Switch Port VLAN Settings
ComputerName  : SERVER4
SettingData   : \\SERVER4\root\virtualization\v2:Msvm_EthernetSwitchPortVlanSettingData.InstanceID="Microsoft:Definitio
                n\\952C5004-4465-451C-8CB8-FA9AB382B773\\Default"

Id            : 998bef4a-5d55-492a-9c43-8b2f5eae9f2b
ExtensionId   : 11EC6134-128A-4A23-B12F-164184B48348
ExtensionName : Microsoft Virtual Ethernet Switch Native Extension
Name          : Ethernet Switch Port ACL Settings
ComputerName  : SERVER4
SettingData   : \\SERVER4\root\virtualization\v2:Msvm_EthernetSwitchPortAclSettingData.InstanceID="Microsoft:Definition
                \\998BEF4A-5D55-492A-9C43-8B2F5EAE9F2B\\Default"
```

The example shown in the preceding screenshot gets all the virtual switch extensions that support switch-level features that can be configured on a virtual switch:

```
PS C:\> Get-VMSystemSwitchExtensionSwitchFeature

Id            : 8b54c928-eb03-4aff-8039-99171dd900ff
ExtensionId   : 11EC6134-128A-4A23-B12F-164184B48348
ExtensionName : Microsoft Virtual Ethernet Switch Native Extension
Name          :  SCVMM Ethernet Switch Feature Internal Settings
ComputerName  : SERVER4
SettingData   : \\SERVER4\root\virtualization\v2:Scvmm_VirtualEthernetSwitchInternalSettingData.InstanceID="Microsoft:D
                efinition\\8B54C928-EB03-4AFF-8039-99171DD900FF\\Default"

Id            : 8e540f36-bdf7-47d3-a99a-7055abe2ff4e
ExtensionId   : 11EC6134-128A-4A23-B12F-164184B48348
ExtensionName : Microsoft Virtual Ethernet Switch Native Extension
Name          : Virtual Ethernet Switch Network Virtualization Settings
ComputerName  : SERVER4
SettingData   : \\SERVER4\root\virtualization\v2:Scvmm_VirtualEthernetSwitchHyperVNetworkVirtualizationSettingData.Inst
                anceID="Microsoft:Definition\\8E540F36-BDF7-47D3-A99A-7055ABE2FF4E\\Default"

Id            : 3eb2b8e8-4abf-4dbf-9071-16dd47481fbe
ExtensionId   : 11EC6134-128A-4A23-B12F-164184B48348
ExtensionName : Microsoft Virtual Ethernet Switch Native Extension
Name          : Ethernet Switch Bandwidth Settings
ComputerName  : SERVER4
SettingData   : \\SERVER4\root\virtualization\v2:Msvm_VirtualEthernetSwitchBandwidthSettingData.InstanceID="Microsoft:D
                efinition\\3EB288E8-4ABF-4D8F-9071-16DD47481FBE\\Default"
```

The example shown in the following screenshot removes a feature configured on the virtual network adapter(s) of a virtual machine:

```
PS C:\>$feature = Get-VMSwitchExtensionPortFeature -VMName VM2 -FeatureId 776e0ba7-94a1-41c8-8f28-951f524251b5
PS C:\>Remove-VMSwitchExtensionPortFeature VM2 -VMSwitchExtensionFeature $feature
```

The example shown in the following screenshot converts a virtual switch named WA to an internal switch:

```
PS C:\> Set-VMSwitch WA -SwitchType Internal
```

The example shown in the following screenshot sets the minimum bandwidth allocation threshold to 500 Mbps on a virtual switch named CA, for all virtual machines without explicit minimum bandwidth configuration:

```
PS C:\> Set-VMSwitch CA -DefaultFlowMinimumBandwidthAbsolute 500000000
```

The example shown in the following screenshot configures a feature on a virtual network adapter on a virtual machine, VM2:

```
PS C:\>$ModifiedFeature = Get-VMSwitchExtensionPortFeature -VMName VM2 -FeatureName "Ethernet Switch Port Security Settings"
PS C:\>$ModifiedFeature.SettingData.EnableDhcpGuard = $false
PS C:\>Set-VMSwitchExtensionPortFeature -VMName VM2 -VMSwitchExtensionFeature $ModifiedFeature
```

The feature shown in the following screenshot configures a feature on a virtual switch, External:

```
PS C:\>$feature = Get-VMSystemSwitchExtensionSwitchFeature -FeatureName "Ethernet Switch Bandwidth Settings"
PS C:\>$feature.SettingData.DefaultFlowReservation = 100000000
PS C:\>Set-VMSwitchExtensionSwitchFeature External $feature
```

Creating and removing Hyper-V virtual switches

Now, let's create a new virtual machine switch for handling **Quality of Service (QoS)** traffic for a Hyper-V host using the `New-VMSwitch` cmdlet. The previous example creates a new QoS switch, which binds to a network adapter called `Team-NIC2-VMNetwork` and supports a weight-based minimum bandwidth:

```
PS C:\Users\Administrator> New-VMSwitch "QoS Switch" -NetAdapterName "Team-NIC2-VMNetwork" -MinimumBandwidthMode Weight

Name        SwitchType NetAdapterInterfaceDescription
----        ---------- ------------------------------
QoS Switch  External   Intel(R) 82580 Gigabit Network Connection #4
```

The example shown in the following screenshot removes a virtual switch named `QoS Switch`:

```
PS C:\>Remove-VMSwitch "QoS Switch"
```

The example shown in the following screenshot renames the virtual switch, `QoS Switch`, as `IIS Switch`:

```
PS C:\>Rename-VMSwitch "QoS Switch" -NewName "IIS Switch"
```

Managing virtual machine migrations

Hyper-V PowerShell cmdlets allow you to move the virtual machine from one host to another. It not only allows you to move only the virtual machine, but also the virtual machine and the associated storage, if needed.

Type the following command to get the list of all cmdlets that can be used to move the virtual machine from one Hyper-V host to another:

```
gcm *move* -Module hyper-v
```

The following screenshot shows the output of the preceding command:

```
PS C:\Users\Administrator> gcm *move* -Module hyper-v

CommandType     Name                ModuleName
-----------     ----                ----------
Cmdlet          Move-VM             Hyper-V
Cmdlet          Move-VMStorage      Hyper-V
```

As you can see, there are two cmdlets present—one to move a virtual machine and the other to move the virtual machine along with the virtual machine storage. The command shown in the following screenshot migrates a live virtual machine live called "New Virtual Machine" to a remote Hyper-V host named server2:

```
PS C:\Users\Administrator> Move-VM "New Virtual Machine" server2
```

The command shown in the following screenshot moves a virtual machine, Test VM, to a remote computer server and places the files associated with the virtual machine in the specified locations under D:\TestVM on the remote computer:

```
PS C:\>Move-VM "Test VM" remoteServer -VirtualMachinePath D:\TestVM\Config -SnapshotFilePath D:\TestVM\Snapshots
-SmartPagingFilePath D:\TestVM\SmartPaging -IncludeStorage -VHDs @(@{"SourceFilePath" = "C:\TestVM\Disk1.VHDX";
"DestinationFilePath" = "D:\TestVM\Disks\Disk1.VHDX"}, @{"SourceFilePath" = "C:\TestVM\Disk2.VHDX";
"DestinationFilePath" = "D:\TestVM\Disks\Disk2.VHDX"})
```

The command shown in the following screenshot moves the virtual machine, Test VM, to the remote computer, remoteServer, and moves all the files associated with the virtual machine to D:\TestVM on the remote computer:

```
PS C:\>Move-VM "Test VM" remoteServer -IncludeStorage -DestinationStoragePath D:\TestVM
```

The command shown in the following screenshot moves all the files associated with a virtual machine, Test VM, to D:\TestVM:

```
PS C:\> Move-VMStorage "Test VM" -DestinationStoragePath D:\TestVM
```

Managing virtual machine imports, exports, and snapshots

Exporting virtual machines allows you to have a backup of the virtual machine that is stored safely at a predefined location and can be later imported if the live VM goes offline or is corrupted. Taking snapshots of virtual machines allows you to create a state as backup of the virtual machine. It also allows the application admin to test configuration changes on a VM after installing an application or applying a hotfix. These differences from the snapshot can be either applied to the virtual machine to go back to a state in time or can be merged with the current state of the virtual machine.

Importing and exporting virtual machines

Using the Hyper-V PowerShell cmdlets, you can either import, export, or take virtual machine snapshots. The `Import-VM` cmdlet imports a virtual machine from a file. The next example shows how you can use this cmdlet to import a virtual machine into your environment.

The following example imports the virtual machine by copying its files to the default virtual machine and the virtual hard drive storage locations of the Hyper-V host. The imported virtual machine will be given a new unique identifier and not the one in the configuration file. This is useful when you want to import multiple copies of a virtual machine since each virtual machine must have a unique identifier. The following screenshot shows how the `Import-VM` cmdlet imports a virtual machine into your environment:

```
PS C:\>Import-VM -Path 'D:\Test2\Virtual Machines\8F148B6D-C674-413E-9FCC-4FBED185C52D.XML' -Copy -GenerateNewId
```

The example shown in the following screenshot imports the virtual machine from its configuration file. The virtual machine is registered in place, so its files are not copied:

```
PS C:\>Import-VM -Path 'D:\Test\VirtualMachines\5AE40946-3A98-428E-8C83-081A3C6BD18C.XML'
```

Importing a virtual machine to a different Hyper-V host can be a bit tricky, as there can be compatibility issues between the destination Hyper-V host and the current Hyper-V host from which the virtual machine was exported.

The following example shows a similar example. Here, we are trying to import a virtual machine, which was exported from a different Hyper-V host. This led to an error, asking us to run the `Compare-VM` cmdlet to find out the virtual machine's incompatibilities with the Hyper-V host:

```
PS C:\>Import-VM -Path 'D:\vm1\Virtual Machines\53EAE599-4D3B-4923-B173-6AEA29CB7F42.XML'
Import-VM : Unable to import virtual machine due to configuration errors.  Please use Compare-VM to repair the
virtual machine.
At line:1 char:1
+ import-vm -Path 'D:\vm1\Virtual Machines\53EAE599-4D3B-4923-B173-6AEA29CB7F42.XM ...
+ ~~~~~~~~~~~~~~~~~~~~~~~~~~~~~~~~~~~~~~~~~~~~~~~~~~~~~~~~~~~~~~~~~~~~~~~~~~~~~~~~~~~
    + CategoryInfo          : NotSpecified: (:) [Import-VM], VirtualizationOperationFailedException
    + FullyQualifiedErrorId : Microsoft.HyperV.PowerShell.Commands.ImportVMCommand
```

Next, we use the `Compare-VM` cmdlet to save the compatibility report:

```
PS C:\>$report = Compare-VM -Path 'D:\vm1\Virtual Machines\53EAE599-4D3B-4923-B173-6AEA29CB7F42.XML'
```

Formatting the compatibility report reveals that the virtual network adapter was connected to the switch, Production, during the export, and the current Hyper-V host has no switch by that name:

```
$report.Incompatibilities | Format-Table -AutoSize
```

The following screenshot displays the output:

```
PS C:\>$report.Incompatibilities | Format-Table -AutoSize
Message                                       MessageId Source
-------                                       --------- ------
Could not find Ethernet switch 'Production'.      33012 Microsoft.HyperV.PowerShell.VMNetworkAdapter
```

Next, we disconnect the network adapter, which caused an error as per the compatibility report. To disconnect the virtual network adapter, run the following cmdlet:

```
$report.Incompatibilities[0].Source | Disconnect-VMNetworkAdapter
```

```
PS C:\>$report.Incompatibilities[0].Source | Disconnect-VMNetworkAdapter
```

Once the incompatibilities are fixed, we again generate a new compatibility report to determine if the virtual machine is compatible with the Hyper-V host:

```
Compare-VM -CompatibilityReport $report
```

```
PS C:\>Compare-VM -CompatibilityReport $report
```

We can see that there are no incompatibility messages in the output of $report:

```
PS C:\>$report
VM                  : Microsoft.HyperV.PowerShell.VirtualMachine
OperationType       : ImportVirtualMachine
Destination         : HYPER-V-1
Path                : D:\vm1\Virtual Machines\53EAE599-4D3B-4923-B173-6AEA29CB7F42.XML
SnapshotPath        : D:\vm1\Snapshots
VhdDestinationPath  :
VhdSourcePath       :
Incompatibilities   :

Imports the virtual machine.
PS C:\>import-vm -CompatibilityReport $report
Name State CPUUsage(%) MemoryAssigned(M) MemoryDemand(M) MemoryStatus Uptime   Status              ReplicationState
---- ----- ----------- ----------------- --------------- ------------ ------   ------              ----------------
VM1  Off   0           0                 0                            00:00:00 Operating normally  Disabled
```

Now, when we try to import the virtual machine whose configuration was not earlier compatible with the Hyper-V host, we see that the virtual machine gets imported successfully:

```
PS C:\>import-vm -CompatibilityReport $report
Name  State CPUUsage(%) MemoryAssigned(M) MemoryDemand(M) MemoryStatus Uptime    Status              ReplicationState
----  ----- ----------- ----------------- --------------- ------------ ------    ------              ----------------
VM1   Off   0           0                 0                            00:00:00  Operating normally  Disabled
```

Similarly, to export a virtual machine, you can use the Export-VM cmdlet. The Export-VM cmdlet exports a virtual machine to disk. This cmdlet creates a folder at a specified location with three subfolders: Snapshots, Virtual Hard Disks, and Virtual Machines. The Snapshots and Virtual Hard Disk folders contain the snapshots and the virtual hard disks of the specified virtual machine respectively. The Virtual Machines folder contains the configuration XML of the specified virtual machine. The example shown in the following screenshot exports the virtual machine, Test, to the root of the D drive:

```
PS C:\Users\Administrator> Export-VM -Name "New Virtual Machine" -Path D:\
PS C:\Users\Administrator>
```

The example shown in the following screenshot exports all the virtual machines to the root of the D drive. Each virtual machine will be exported to its own folder:

```
PS C:\>Get-VM | Export-VM -Path D:\
```

Managing virtual machine snapshots

The virtual machine snapshot nomenclature in PowerShell has been changed to Checkpoint-VM. To get the list of all cmdlets that can be used to checkpoint a VM, type the command shown in the following screenshot in a PowerShell prompt:

```
PS C:\Users\Administrator> gcm *checkpoint* -Module hyper-v

CommandType     Name                                               ModuleName
-----------     ----                                               ----------
Cmdlet          Checkpoint-VM                                      Hyper-V
```

Let's start exploring some of these cmdlets. Let's start with the cmdlet, which allows you to take a VM snapshot of the `Checkpoint-VM` cmdlet. The `Checkpoint-VM` cmdlet creates a snapshot of a virtual machine. Type the command shown in the following screenshot in a PowerShell prompt to checkpoint a VM.

The command shown in the following screenshot checks the virtual machine, `Test`, on the Hyper-V host, `Server1`, and creates a snapshot of it:

```
PS C:\>Get-VM Test -ComputerName Server1 | Checkpoint-VM
```

Another example of checkpointing a VM is shown in the following command line:

```
CheckpointVM -Name Test -Computername Server1 -
  Snapshotname "My New Snapshot"
```

There are a number of cmdlets, which are available to manage the virtual machine snapshots. To get a list of all the cmdlets that can be used to manage the virtual machine snapshots, type the command shown in the following screenshot in a PowerShell prompt:

```
PS C:\Users\Administrator> gcm *snapshot* -Module hyper-v

CommandType     Name                           ModuleName
-----------     ----                           ----------
Cmdlet          Export-VMSnapshot              Hyper-V
Cmdlet          Get-VMSnapshot                 Hyper-V
Cmdlet          Remove-VMSnapshot              Hyper-V
Cmdlet          Rename-VMSnapshot              Hyper-V
Cmdlet          Restore-VMSnapshot             Hyper-V
```

The example shown in the following screenshot exports a snapshot, `Base Image`, of the virtual machine, `TestVM`, to `D:\`:

```
PS C:\>Export-VMSnapshot -Name 'Base Image' -VMName TestVM -Path D:\
```

The example shown in the following screenshot gets all the snapshots of the virtual machine, `TestVM`:

```
PS C:\>Get-VMSnapshot -VMName TestVM
```

The example shown in the following screenshot gets all the standard snapshots of the virtual machine, TestVM:

```
PS C:\>Get-VM -Name TestVM | Get-VMSnapshot -SnapshotType Standard
```

The example shown in the following screenshot gets the immediate parent of a snapshot before applying the updates to the virtual machine, TestVM:

```
PS C:\>$snapshot = Get-VMSnapshot -Name 'Before applying updates' -VMName TestVM

PS C:\>Get-VMSnapshot -ParentOf $snapshot
```

The example shown in the following screenshot gets the immediate child snapshots of $snapshot before applying updates to the virtual machine, TestVM:

```
PS C:\>$snapshot = Get-VMSnapshot -Name 'Before applying updates' -VMName TestVM

PS C:\>Get-VMSnapshot -ChildOf $snapshot
```

The example shown in the following screenshot deletes all the snapshots of the virtual machine, TestVM, whose names start with Experiment:

```
PS C:\>Get-VM TestVM | Remove-VMSnapshot -Name Experiment*
```

Note that removing a snapshot takes a little while, depending on how old the snapshot is and how much data has changed between the dates of the merge. The following example deletes all the snapshots of the virtual machine, TestVM, that are older than 90 days:

```
PS C:\>Get-VMSnapshot -VMName TestVM | Where-Object {$_.CreationTime -lt (Get-Date).AddDays(-90) } |
Remove-VMSnapshot
```

The example shown in the following screenshot renames the snapshot, `Configuration 2`, of the virtual machine, `TestVM`, to `Configuration 2: applied all updates`:

```
PS C:\>Rename-VMSnapshot -VMName TestVM -Name "Configuration 2" -NewName "Configuration 2: applied all updates"
```

The example shown in the following screenshot restores the snapshot, `Base image`, of the virtual machine, `TestVM`:

```
PS C:\>Restore-VMSnapshot -Name 'Base image' -VMName TestVM
Confirm
Are you sure you want to perform this action?
Restore-VMSnapshot will restore snapshot "Base image".
[Y] Yes  [A] Yes to All  [N] No  [L] No to All  [S] Suspend  [?] Help
(default is "Y"): Y
```

The example shown in the following screenshot applies the most recent snapshot to all the virtual machines with no confirmation prompts:

```
PS C:\>Get-VM | Foreach-Object { $_ | Get-VMSnapshot | Sort CreationTime | Select -Last 1 | Restore-VMSnapshot -Confirm:$false }
```

Managing virtual machine backups with Hyper-V Replica

Hyper-V Replica was a new feature introduced in Windows Server 2012. In Windows 2012 R2, some new enhancements were introduced into Hyper-V Replica, which include the replica frequency throttling and the feature to extend the replica.

The example shown in the following screenshot configures the replication of `testvm` on the local Hyper-V host and directs replication traffic to port 80 on a replica server named `server04.test.com`, using Kerberos as the type of authentication:

```
PS C:\> Enable-VMReplication -VMName testvm -ComputerName server04.test.com 80 kerberos
```

The example shown in the following screenshot configures the replication of all the virtual machines on the local Hyper-V host and directs replication traffic to port 80 on a replica server named `server04.test.com`, using Kerberos as the type of authentication:

```
PS C:\> Enable-VMReplication * -ComputerName server04.test.com 80 kerberos_
```

The example shown in the following screenshot gets the replication settings of all the replication-enabled virtual machines on the local Hyper-V host:

```
PS C:\>Get-VMReplication
```

The example shown in the following screenshot gets the replication settings of all the virtual machines in the Replicating state:

```
PS C:\>Get-VMReplication -ReplicationState Replicating
```

The example shown in the following screenshot gets the replication configuration of the local replica server:

```
PS C:\> Get-VMReplicationServer
```

The example shown in the following screenshot imports the initial replication files for a virtual machine named VM01 from the location, d:\VMImportLocation\VM01:

```
PS C:\>Import-VMInitialReplication VM01 d:\VMImportLocation\VM01
```

The example shown in the following screenshot gets the replication monitoring details of a virtual machine named VM01:

```
PS C:\>Measure-VMReplication VM01
```

The example shown in the following screenshot gets the replication monitoring details of all the virtual machines that have a replication health as Warning:

```
PS C:\> Measure-VMReplication -ReplicationHealth Warning
```

Virtual machine replication can be removed by using the `Remove-VMReplication` cmdlet. The example shown in the following screenshot removes the replication relationships from all the replication-enabled virtual machines on the local Hyper-V host:

```
PS C:\>Remove-VMReplication *
```

The example shown in the following screenshot resets the replication statistics of all the replication-enabled virtual machines on the local Hyper-V host:

```
PS C:\>Get-VMReplication | Reset-VMReplicationStatistics
```

The example shown in the following screenshot resynchronizes replication of the virtual machine, VM01:

```
PS C:\>Resume-VMReplication VM01 -Resynchronize
```

The example shown in the following screenshot schedules the resynchronization of the replication for the virtual machine, VM01, to start at 5:00 AM on August 1, 2012:

```
PS C:\>Resume-VMReplication VM01 -Resynchronize -ResynchronizeStartTime "8/1/2012 05:00 AM"
```

The example shown in the following screenshot configures the recovery history and the application-consistent recovery points of the virtual machine, VM01:

```
PS C:\> Set-VMReplication VM01 -RecoveryHistory 4 -VSSSnapshotFrequency 4
```

The example shown in the following screenshot reverses the replication of the virtual machine, VM01:

```
PS C:\> Set-VMReplication VM01 -Reverse
```

The example shown in the following screenshot configures the local host as a replica server and specifies Kerberos for authentication:

```
Set-VMReplicationServer $true –AllowedAuthenticationType Kerberos
```

```
PS C:\> Set-VMReplicationServer $true –AllowedAuthenticationType Kerberos
```

The example shown in the following screenshot starts initial replication over the network for all the virtual machines on the local Hyper-V host for which the initial replication is pending:

```
PS C:\>Start-VMInitialReplication *
```

The example shown in the following screenshot starts initial replication over the network for the virtual machines whose destination path is mentioned, on the local Hyper-V host for which initial replication is pending:

```
PS C:\>Start-VMInitialReplication * -DestinationPath R:\IRLoc
```

The example shown in the following screenshot stops the initial replication of all the virtual machines whose initial replication is in progress on the local replica server:

```
PS C:\>Stop-VMInitialReplication *
```

The example shown in the following screenshot stops all ongoing replications of virtual machines on the local Hyper-V server:

```
PS C:\>Stop-VMReplication *
```

The example shown in the following screenshot suspends replication of all virtual machines on the local Hyper-V host:

```
PS C:\>Suspend-VMReplication *
```

Throttling the Hyper-V Replica traffic involves changing the port used for the Hyper-V Replica from the default 80 to 443 (which can be done in the GUI or via Windows PowerShell). Then, use QoS to limit bandwidth at different times of the day for that port. This effectively throttles the transmission of the write logs.

We need to use the NetQoS policy to throttle the replica traffic; this can be done via PowerShell using the `New-NetQosPolicy` cmdlet. Based on the destination port (the port on which the replica server has been configured to receive replication traffic — maybe it's port 80 in your case) or the destination subnet, you can specify a throttling value, `(-ThrottleRateActionBitsPerSecond)`, or assign a weight, `MinBandwidthWeightAction`.

The `New-NetQosPolicy` cmdlet creates a new network QoS policy. A QoS policy consists of two main parts: match conditions (also known as filters) and actions. Match conditions such as the name by which an application is run on Windows Server 2012 and later versions or a TCP port number decide to what traffic the policy is relating. Parameters such as `DSCPAction` and `ThrottleRateAction` determine how the policy will handle the matched traffic. Besides match conditions and actions, there are also some general parameters such as `NetworkProfile` and `Precedence` that the users can customize for a QoS policy. These are shown in the following screenshot:

```
PS C:\Users\Administrator> New-NetQosPolicy "Replica traffic to 8080" -DestinationPort 8080 -ThrottleRateActionBitsPerSe
cond 100000

Name            : Replica traffic to 8080
Owner           : Group Policy (Machine)
NetworkProfile  : All
Precedence      : 127
IPProtocol      : Both
IPDstPortStart  : 8080
IPDstPortEnd    : 8080
ThrottleRate    : 100 KBits/sec
```

The illustrated solution of replica shown in the preceding screenshot throttling would be to limit traffic based on the destination port. In this case, all the traffic from the Hyper-V host to a specific destination port gets throttled.

Windows 2012 R2 introduced some major enhancements in Hyper-V Replica. A new feature is extended replication. In extended replication, your replica server forwards changes that occur on the primary virtual machines to a third server — the extended replica server. After a planned or unplanned failover from the primary server to the replica server, the extended replica server provides further business continuity protection. You can configure extended replication by using the `-Extended` option in Windows PowerShell.

Managing virtual machine connections

With Windows Server 2012 R2 Hyper-V, Hyper-V is able to redirect local resources to a virtual machine session using the Virtual Machine Connection tool. This enhanced session mode connection uses the remote desktop connection session via the virtual machine bus (VMBus). Therefore, the network connectivity to the virtual machine is not required.

Let's look at the cmdlets that will be used to manage the virtual machine connect feature:

```
PS C:\Users\Administrator> gcm *vmconnect* -Module hyper-v

CommandType     Name                            ModuleName
-----------     ----                            ----------
Cmdlet          Get-VMConnectAccess             Hyper-V
Cmdlet          Grant-VMConnectAccess           Hyper-V
Cmdlet          Revoke-VMConnectAccess          Hyper-V
```

The preceding command gets a list of all the users who have access to connect to any virtual machine on the local computer. The following example assumes that the Grant-VMConnectAccess cmdlet has been run previously for at least one user account:

```
PS C:\>Get-VMConnectAccess
```

The command shown in the following screenshot provides a user with virtual\administrator access to connect to a virtual machine named exchange1:

```
PS C:\> Get-VMConnectAccess -VMName exchange1 -UserName virtual\administrator
```

The command shown in the following screenshot revokes the access of user, virtual\administrator, to connect to a virtual machine named exchange1:

```
PS C:\> Revoke-VMConnectAccess -VMName exchange1 -UserName virtual\administrator
PS C:\> _
```

Summary

In this chapter, we covered some of the most commonly used administrative tasks and saw the PowerShell way of automating them. In the next chapter, we will look at ways to create reusable PowerShell scripts for day-to-day Hyper-V management activities using the cmdlet concepts that you learned in the previous and current chapters.

4
Creating Reusable PowerShell Scripts Using Hyper-V PowerShell Module Cmdlets

In this chapter, we will look at how to create reusable PowerShell scripts for day-to-day Hyper-V management activities using cmdlets. We will be utilizing the core cmdlets that we learned in the previous two chapters to create these reusable scripts. We have subdivided this chapter into four sections, which will cover the core automation strategies that can be used to manage repetitive administrative tasks:

- Creating reusable scripts for virtual machine creation utilizing **offloaded data transfers (ODX)**
- Creating reusable scripts for virtual machine live migration
- Creating reusable scripts to manage a virtual machine's snapshots, export, and import
- Creating reusable scripts to automate installation of Integration Service in virtual machines

Creating reusable scripts for virtual machine creation utilizing ODX

Using the core virtual machine cmdlets included in Hyper-V PowerShell, we can automate the process of virtual machine creation. With Windows Server 2012, Windows Server 2012 R2, and System Center Virtual Machine Manager 2012 R2, we can speed up the process of virtual machine provisioning utilizing ODX, so let's look at what exactly ODX is.

ODX is a new technology feature supported by the latest Windows Server 2012 and Windows Server 2012 R2 operating systems that offloads the standard copy operations from Windows networks to the underlying storage system. For example, a virtual hard disk, when copied over the network for a virtual machine provisioning process, would take hours to complete the copy process depending on the virtual hard disk size as the copy process takes place over the network.

ODX is enabled by default in Windows Server 2012 and Windows Server 2012 R2. You can check whether it's enabled or disabled using a simple registry key check using PowerShell:

1. In a PowerShell prompt with administrative rights, execute the following command:

   ```
   Get-ItemProperty hklm:\system\currentcontrolset\control\
       filesystem -Name "FilterSupportedFeaturesMode"
   ```

   As you can see, when we execute this command on the test server, it shows that ODX is disabled since the value is set to one:

```
[            ]: PS C:\ClusterStorage\Volume1> Get-ItemProperty hklm:\system\currentcontrolset\control\filesystem -Name "F
ilterSupportedFeaturesMode"

FilterSupportedFeaturesMode : 1
PSPath                      : Microsoft.PowerShell.Core\Registry::HKEY_LOCAL_MACHINE\system\currentcontrolset\control\f
                              ilesystem
PSParentPath                : Microsoft.PowerShell.Core\Registry::HKEY_LOCAL_MACHINE\system\currentcontrolset\control
PSChildName                 : filesystem
PSDrive                     : HKLM
PSProvider                  : Microsoft.PowerShell.Core\Registry
```

2. Now, to enable ODX, we need to set this registry key value to 0.

3. Execute the following PowerShell command to enable ODX:

```
Set-ItemProperty hklm:\system\currentcontrolset\
    control\filesystem -Name "FilterSupportedFeaturesMode"
    -Value 0 -Type Dword
```

4. Now, let's explore a PowerShell script that you can reuse in your environment to automate the creation of virtual machines using ODX. We will be using the concept of PowerShell remoting to do this. We have explained the various cmdlets in the following code, which when executed together as a PowerShell script will help you to automate the virtual machine provisioning process. I have broken the script into small sections explaining in detail what each cmdlet is expected to do when it is executed:

   ° Enter the following command in a PowerShell window:

```
###########################################################
#Create Credential Objects to Connect to the Hyper-V Host
###########################################################
$password = Read Host -AsSecureString

$credential = New-Object
    System.Management.Automation.PsCredential
    ("HVHOST\admin",$password)
```

Using the preceding piece of code, we created a variable called $password into which we saved a predefined password to a secure string using the ConvertTo-SecureString cmdlet. Once we created a secured password, we created a $credential variable that contains the credential object. This way of accepting credentials allows the administrator to save the credentials in a variable that can be reused, and it avoids the usage of the Get-Credential cmdlet, which gives a pop up every time a user tries to authenticate to a system or the Hyper-V host:

○ In this section, we will create a remote PowerShell session to the Hyper-V host using the credentials that we saved in the `$credential` variable. We will also use the CredSSP-based authentication mechanism:

```
###########################################################
#Create PowerShell Remote sessions to the Hyper-V Host
###########################################################
$session = New-PSSession -ComputerName
  <Hyper-V Host Name> -credential $credential
Invoke-Command -Session $session -ScriptBlock {
```

○ In this section, we will create a new directory using the `New-Item` cmdlet to save the virtual machine in a clustered shared storage location; this will contain the virtual machine configuration file and its virtual hard disk:

```
###########################################################
#Create a New directory to save the virtual machine contents
###########################################################

New-Item -Path "C:\ClusterStorage\Volume1\VMS" -
  Name <Virtual Machine Name> -ItemType directory -Force
```

○ In this section, we will use the magic of ODX by copying over the virtual machine hard disk to the destination virtual machine location using the `Copy-Item` cmdlet. Now, as I have ODX enabled, the `Copy-Item` cmdlet copies across the virtual machines super-fast to the destination location utilizing the underlying storage technologies:

```
#############################################################
##########
#Use ODX based copy process to copy across the VHD in
seconds
#############################################################
#######################
Copy-Item "C:\ClusterStorage\Volume1\vhd\
  win2k12r2_sysprepped.vhdx" "C:\ClusterStorage\Volume1\VMS\
  <Virtual Machine Name>"
```

○ In this section, we will change the current directory to the location where we copied over the virtual machine hard disk. We will rename the virtual hard disk to a more user friendly name, which will consist of the virtual machine's name for easy administration, using the Set-Location cmdlet:

```
Set-Location "C:\ClusterStorage\Volume1\VMS\
    <Virtual Machine Name>"

$VMPath = "C:\ClusterStorage\Volume1\VMS\
    <Virtual Machine Name>"

Rename-Item win2k12r2_sysprepped.vhdx -NewName "
    <Virtual Machine Name>-OS.vhdx"
```

○ In this section, we will create the virtual machine using the New-VM cmdlet and assign the virtual machine a memory of 4 GB and the virtual machine hard disk path and virtual machine path of $VHDPath and $VMPath respectively, and also a virtual switch named "Virtual Switch V1":

```
################################################################
##################
#Create Virtual Machine on the Hyper-V host and Configure
its
    properties
################################################################
##################
Import-Module hyper-v


$VHDPath = "C:\ClusterStorage\Volume1\ VMS\
    <Virtual Machine Name>/"<Virtual Machine Name>-OS.vhdx "


New-VM -ComputerName $PH -MemoryStartupBytes 4GB -Name
    <Virtual Machine Name>-VHDPath $VHDPath -Path $VMPath
    -SwitchName "Virtual Switch V1"



################################################################
############################
#Set Vm properties before start, enable dynamic memory
    for memory optimization
```

```
Set-VM -name <Virtual Machine Name>-ProcessorCount 4 -
    DynamicMemory -AutomaticStartAction StartIfRunning -
    AutomaticStopAction Save


##############################################################
##############################
# Disable Time Sync on a VM so that it sync's time from
    a domain controller
Disable-VMIntegrationService -VMName <Virtual Machine
    Name> -Name "Time Synchronization"
```

Start-VM <Virtual Machine Name> -Verbose

Once the virtual machine gets created, we can use the Set-VM cmdlet to set the virtual machine properties such as processor count, dynamic memory, and the automatic start and stop action. We will also disable the "Time Synchronization" VM Integration Service so that the virtual machine does not sync its clock with the time set on the Hyper-V host. Once all the configuration activities are completed, we will start the virtual machine using the Start-VM cmdlet:

```
######################################################################
##################
#Make the Virtual Machines Highly Available and add them to the
clustered instance
######################################################################
##################
Import-Module failoverclusters
```

**Add-ClusterVirtualMachineRole -VirtualMachine <Virtual Machine
Name>**

5. Next, we will make the virtual machine highly available using the Add-ClusterVirtualMachineRole cmdlet so that its services remain highly available in the event of a host Hyper-V virtual machine crash.

Creating reusable scripts for virtual machine live migration

Reusable scripts help the Hyper-V administrator to automate various mundane tasks. Let's explore ways to automate one of the most commonly used virtual machine tasks. To do this, let's look at a script that can be used to automate the live migration of virtual machines across various Hyper-V hosts in a cluster.

Similar to the previous script, let's break this script into various components to understand its execution step by step. Also, in the scripting technique illustrated as follows, we will be using the concept of PowerShell workflows to migrate the virtual machines across the Hyper-V host cluster live in a parallel manner and not a sequential one:

```
workflow Move-LiveVM

{

param(
[Parameter(Mandatory)]
[string]$SourceHyperVhost,
[Parameter(Mandatory)]
[string]$DestinationHyperVhost,
[Parameter(Mandatory)]
[string]$ClusterName

)
```

Using the preceding piece of code, we created a PowerShell workflow called `Move-LiveVM`, which gets its input from the `$SourceHyperVhost` (which is the source Hyper-V host name), `$DestinationHyperVhost` (which is the destination Hyper-V host name), and `$clustername` (which is the Hyper-V cluster name) parameters. All these are mandatory parameters and need to be input passed by the user during workflow execution:

```
$vminfo = Get-ClusterGroup -cluster $clustername | Where-Object
-filterscript {$_.grouptype -match "VirtualMachine" -and $_.ownernode
-match $SourceHyperVhost}



Foreach -parallel  ($vm in $vminfo)



{



Move-ClusterVirtualMachineRole $vm -Node $DestinationHyperVhost
-MigrationType live  -Cluster $clustername



}



}
```

Next, we extracted the virtual machine cluster group name for all the virtual machines that were highly available and used a for-each loop with the – parallel parameter to move the virtual machines to the destination Hyper-V host using live migration in parallel.

Creating reusable scripts to manage export and import of virtual machine snapshots

Next, we will look at some scripts that can be used to automate the virtual machine import, export, and snapshot processes. This section is relatively simple as we will be using a for-each loop to iterate across all virtual machines and perform these activities.

For this particular example, we will be using a single script to illustrate all three processes:

```
$vminfo = Get-VM
```

As you can see in the preceding piece of code, we will extract the information about all the virtual machines and store it in a variable, $vminfo:

```
Foreach ($vm in $vminfo)

{
```

Next, let's iterate across all the virtual machines stored in the $vminfo variable and create a snapshot of the virtual machines using the Checkpoint-VM cmdlet:

```
Checkpoint-VM -Name $vm.name -SnapshotName BeforeInstallingUpdates
}
```

Next, let's export all the virtual machines to a location using the Export-VM cmdlet. We can use a similar for-loop technique to export all the virtual machines in our Hyper-V server to a predefined location:

```
$vminfo = Get-VM

Foreach ($vm in $vminfo)

{

Export-VM -Name $vm.name -Path D:\Export

}
```

Once we export all these virtual machines to a predefined location, we can also import them using the Import-VM cmdlet. We can again use a similar for loop technique to import the virtual machines:

```
$vminfo=GET-CHILDITEM D:\Export -recurse -include *.exp
```

Through the preceding piece of code, we can get the details of all the virtual machines that have been exported in our example:

```
$VMinfo | FOREACH {

IMPORT-VM -path $_.Fullname -Copy -VhdDestinationPath
  $VMDefaultDrive -

VirtualMachinePath $VMDefaultPath -SnapshotFilePath
  $VMDefaultPath -SmartPagingFilePath $VMDefaultPath -GenerateNewId

}
```

In the preceding code snippet, we iterate across all the virtual machines that have been exported and import them into Hyper-V Manager from the exports.

Creating reusable scripts to automate installation of Integration Service in virtual machines

Next, we will look at some scripts that can be used to automate the installation of Integration Service in virtual machines. These scripts support Windows Server 2012, Hyper-V Version 3, and their later versions from the perspective of Microsoft hypervisor.

This example is illustrated as follows by creating a function that gets Integration Service installed.

Let's consider four parameters for this function, which include the virtual machine name, the Hyper-V hostname, the username, and the password:

```
function Install-VMIntegrationService
{
    [CmdletBinding()]

    Param
    (
      # Param1 help description
      [Parameter(Mandatory=$true,ValueFromPipelineByPropertyName=
        $true,Position=0)]
        $VMName,


        # Param2 help description
        [Parameter(Mandatory=$true,
          ValueFromPipelineByPropertyName=$true,Position=1)]
      $VMComputerName,


        # Param2 help description
        [Parameter(Mandatory=$true,
          ValueFromPipelineByPropertyName=$true,Position=2)]
```

```
    $username,


        # Param2 help description
    [Parameter(Mandatory=$true,
        ValueFromPipelineByPropertyName=$true,Position=3)]
    $password


    )
```

Next, let's iterate across all the virtual machines and their associated Hyper-V host using multiple for-each loops. Consider four parameters for this function, which include the virtual machine name, the Hyper-V hostname, the username, and the password:

```
foreach ($vm in $vmname)


    {


        foreach ($comp in $VMComputerName)


    {
```

Next, we will create a credential object, which will be used to invoke remote PowerShell sessions in the virtual machines to get the Integration Service version.

```
    $pass =  ConvertTo-SecureString  -String $password -
        AsPlainText -force
    $cred = New-Object System.Management.
        Automation.PsCredential($username,$pass)
```

Next, we will mount the VMGuest.iso image to a virtual machine and compare the versions of Integration Service on the Hyper-V host and the virtual machine. I also extract the DVD drive letter:

```
    Set-VMDvdDrive -VMName $vm -Path
"C:\Windows\System32\vmguest.iso"


    $DVDDriveLetter = Get-VMDvdDrive -VMName $vm | select -
        ExpandProperty id | Split-Path -Leaf
```

```
$HostICversion= Get-ItemProperty
  "HKLM:\SOFTWARE\Microsoft\Windows
  NT\CurrentVersion\Virtualization\GuestInstaller\
  Version" | select -ExpandProperty Microsoft-Hyper-V
  -Guest-Installer


$VMICversion = Invoke-Command -ScriptBlock {Get-ItemProperty
  "HKLM:\software\microsoft\virtual machine\
  auto" | select -ExpandProperty integrationservicesversion } -
  ComputerName $comp -Credential $cred
```

If we find that the versions of Integration Service on both the virtual machine and the Hyper-V host are the same, then we will unmount the VMGuest.iso DVD drive from the virtual machine, exit the script, and write a verbose message to the user informing him or her that the Integration Service version is up-to-date on the virtual machine:

```
if($HostICversion -eq $VMICversion) {


Write-Verbose "Hyper-V Host IC Version and the VM $vm IC Version
  are the same" -Verbose


$obj = New-Object psobject -Property @{


'HostIntegration Services Version' =  $HostICversion

'VMIntegration Services Version' =  $VMICversion

'Hyper-V Host Name' = hostname

'VirtualMachine Name'= $vm

}


Write-Output $obj


Set-VMDvdDrive -VMName $vm -ControllerNumber1 -
  ControllerLocation 0 -Path $null


}
```

If we find that the versions of Integration Service on both the virtual machine and the Hyper-V host are different, we will display a message to the user stating that the virtual machine has the old version of Integration Service:

```
else {

    $VMICversion = Invoke-Command -ScriptBlock {Get-ItemProperty
    "HKLM:\software\microsoft\virtual machine\auto" | select
-ExpandProperty integrationservicesversion } -ComputerName $comp
-Credential $cred
    write-verbose  "$vm Old Integration Services Version
    $VMICversion" -Verbose
```

Next, we will use the `Invoke-WMIMethod` cmdlet to install Integration Service silently on the virtual machine; we will allow this command to enter sleep mode for 3 seconds before execution:

```
Invoke-WmiMethod -ComputerName $comp -Class Win32_Process -Name
Create -ArgumentList "$($DVDriveLetter):\support\x86\setup.exe /
quiet /norestart" -Credential $cred



    start-sleep 3
```

Next, we will use a `while` loop to check whether the process that started at the time of the installation of Integration Service was completed successfully; we will also display a message showing the progress of installation:

```
    while (@(Get-Process setup -computername $comp   -ErrorAction
SilentlyContinue).Count -ne 0) {
        Start-Sleep 3
        Write-verbose "Waiting for Integration Service Install to
            Finish on $comp ..." -Verbose
    }
```

Once the script verifies that Integration Service has been installed, we will have to restart the computer for the changes to take place. In the end, we will again compare the Integration Service version on both the virtual machine and the Hyper-V host, verify that it is the same, and give a user friendly output to the user stating the installation has been completed:

```
    write-verbose  "Completed the Installation of Integration
        Services" -Verbose
```

```
    write-verbose  "Restarting Computer for Changes to Take Place"
-Verbose




    Restart-Computer -ComputerName $comp -Wait -For WinRM -Force
-Credential $cred



    write-verbose  "$vm Is Online Now" -Verbose

    $VMICversion = Invoke-Command -ScriptBlock {Get-
      ItemProperty "HKLM:\software\microsoft\virtual
      machine\auto" | select -ExpandProperty
      integrationservicesversion } -ComputerName $comp
      -Credential $cred

    write-verbose  "$vm New Integration Services Version
      $VMICversion" -Verbose


    Set-VMDvdDrive -VMName $vm -ControllerNumber 1 -
      ControllerLocation 0 -Path $null




        }




        }




    }




}
```

Summary

In this chapter, we went in-depth into ways to build custom scripts for various day-to-day administrative activities. In the next chapter, we will cover in detail how to troubleshoot Hyper-V environment issues using the best practices for PowerShell cmdlets in Hyper-V.

5
The Next Step – Integration with SCVMM

The **System Center Virtual Machine Manager** (**SCVMM**) comes with several built-in PowerShell cmdlets that allow one to manage the Hyper-V environment, which is deployed at a very large scale. In this chapter, we will look at how to integrate our existing Hyper-V infrastructure with SCVMM, which is an enterprise-level Microsoft application that allows you to manage multiple Hyper-V environments and provides you with a **single pane of glass** management experience.

We have subdivided this chapter into two sections, which will give you an insight into the advantages of integration with SCVMM and also give you details on the PowerShell cmdlets that you will get after integration with SCVMM:

- Why integrate with SCVMM?
- The new PowerShell cmdlets after integration with SCVMM

Why integrate with SCVMM?

SCVMM 2012 R2 does not just manage **virtual machines** (**VM**) anymore. It does more than that and manages the entire virtualized data center, effectively managing the entire *VM host lifecycle*. SCVMM 2012 R2 can now communicate with bare metal machines with no installed operating system, execute bare metal virtualization, and manage and deploy Hyper-V clusters as well as talk directly to SAN storage. SCVMM allows you to manage an entire cloud—you can now abstract the host, storage, and networking into a unified pool of computing resources.

SCVMM has the ability to deploy the App-V server and deploy the virtualized applications to hosts as well as enabling the SQL server profiles to deploy customized database servers. App-V allows you to stream your applications and allows the administrator to provide software as a service. It can also be centrally managed via the App-V management console. SQL Server profiles in SCVMM allow you to create a profile to deploy a SQL Server instance on a virtual machine.

Overall, the SCVMM features can be categorized into fabrics and services and clouds:

- The fabric feature can be subcategorized into core fabric management, resource optimization, and infrastructure enhancements
- The services and clouds feature includes the cloud management features

Core fabric management

The core fabric management feature gives you the ability to manage all your hardware resources, which include bare metal provisioning and network and storage management. It also enables you to manage multiple hypervisors such as Hyper-V, VMware, and Citrix. Fabric management refers to managing all the features that are necessary to manage VMs. The core fabric management feature consists of three main subcomponents, which are the compute, network and storage resources:

- **The compute resource**: This resource allows one to manage multiple hypervisor platforms, server hardware such as iLO and IPMI, bare metal provisioning with cluster creation, and storage provisioning.

- **The network resource**: This resource allows one to define a logical network with VLANs and subnets per data center location, and assign IP and MAC addresses from pools. It also allows the automated provisioning of load balancers.

- **The storage resource**: This resource allows the infrastructure administrator to do storage provisioning and management using SMI-S, allows it to discover the storage-device-to-VM relationship and classify storage according to its capability. This also allows the administrator to discover and provide new LUNs and assign new storage using Hyper-V hosts and clusters, and also caters to rapid provisioning using LUN cloning.

Resource optimization

The resource optimization feature allows the infrastructure administrator to run his or her Hyper-V environment at optimal settings, which include selecting the right power settings for the Hyper-V hosts using core parking, PRO integration with **System Center Operations Manager (SCOM)**, and also dynamic optimization to proactively monitor the load of the VMs across the cluster.

The Resource optimization feature can be subdivided into three main subcomponents, which are listed as follows:

- **Placement**: This uses the star rating technique to optimally place the VMs on the right hosts. SCVMM has more than 100 placement checks for placing the VMs. It also supports custom placement rules and also its private cloud aware.

- **Dynamic optimization**: The Dynamic optimization feature does not require the pro-pack and, hence, has no dependency on SCOM. This feature manages the cluster level workload balancing scheme for better VM performance, and it utilizes live VM migration to move VM workloads. Dynamic optimizations can be set on manual and automatic modes.

- **Power optimization**: This feature effectively monitors the server that is being utilized and can power off the server during low levels of resource utilization. The administrator has the control to define a power optimization policy. The Power optimization feature is internally dependent on dynamic optimization.

Infrastructure enhancements

The infrastructure enhancement feature includes the new feature of **highly available (HA)** VMM servers, update management, and also extensive PowerShell support. The infrastructure enhancements feature can be subdivided into three main subcomponents, which are PowerShell, HA VMM server, and update management:

- **PowerShell**: SCVMM 2012 R2 is fully PowerShell v3 compatible. It is easily discoverable and also supports backward compatibility with the SCVMM 2008 R2 scripting interface.

- **HA VMM server**: SCVMM 2012 R2 is cluster-aware and hence, supports high availability. This feature effectively eliminates VMM server as a single point of failure.

- **Update management**: The update management feature allows the administrator to update the cluster in an orchestrated manner. Administrators can define baselines and control the update life cycle, which includes on demand scan and remediation. This feature is fully integrated with **Windows Server Update Services (WSUS)**.

Cloud management

Next, let's look at the features that come under cloud management. Cloud management allows the administrator to manage everything in a private cloud environment, which includes managing the network resources in private cloud and delegating self-service provisioning capabilities that allow to author deploy and manage the virtual machines in the private cloud.

The resource cloud management feature can be subdivided into two main subcomponents, which are the cloud capacity and capability profiles and delegation and quota.

- **Cloud capacity and capability profiles**: A cloud can host highly available VMs, allow the virtual machines to use dynamic and differencing disks, and also allow to enable network optimizations. It also allows you to dimension the VMs as per the cloud capacity, which includes setting the number of vCPUs, memory, storage, and the number of deployed VMs.

- **Delegation and quota**: SCVMM allows the administrator to define scopes. The scopes can be subdivided into three types including the everything scope. The everything scope cannot be modified and it can perform any administrative action. The everything scope is owned by the VMM administrator. Next, we have the scope set for host groups and clouds. This scope consists of the delegated and the read-only administrator. This scope allows us to set up fabric by configuring hosts, network, and storage. It allows us to create a cloud and assign it to self-service users. The final scope is the clouds-only scope. A self-service user forms a part of this scope. This scope allows us to deploy and manage VMs and services and also to author the templates. The quotas are set as per user limits.

I hope you have a good understanding on the effectiveness of using SCVMM 2012 R2 to manage a Hyper-V infrastructure. Next, let's look at the new PowerShell cmdlets that come with SCVMM 2012 R2.

PowerShell cmdlets in integration with SCVMM

System Center Virtual Machine Manager 2012 R2 has enormous PowerShell support. Every task that you can perform on the SCVMM console can also be performed using PowerShell. Also, there are some tasks in SCVMM that can only be performed using PowerShell.

There are two ways in which you can access the PowerShell console for SCVMM:

- The first technique is to launch it from the SCVMM console itself. Open the SCVMM console in administrator mode and click on the PowerShell icon in the GUI console. This will launch the PowerShell console with the imported `virtualmachinemanager` PowerShell module:

- You can also import the `virtualmachinemanager` PowerShell module using the `Import-module` cmdlet. Launch the PowerShell console in an administrative mode and type the following command:

```
Import-module virtualmachinemanager
```

This will import the cmdlets in the `virtualmachinemanager` module for administrative use. As you can see in the following screenshot, if I execute a `Measure-Object` cmdlet, PowerShell gives me 619 cmdlets that are available for Hyper-V infrastructure management:

New PowerShell cmdlets have been added to all features in SCVMM, which include networking, virtual machines, and cloud and storage management. So, let's look at some of these cmdlets and their examples:

- `New-SCVirtualMachine`: The `New-SCVirtualMachine` cmdlet allows you to create a new virtual machine. The virtual machine can be created either from a stopped virtual machine or a virtual machine template, which exists on a library host. It can also be created from a **virtual hard disk (VHD)** that contains third-party operating system.

  The following sample code shows how you can create a highly available virtual machine:

```
# We create a Job guid here which is unique per virtual machine
created using
    the below set of cmdlets.
$JobGuid = [System.Guid]::NewGuid().ToString()

# Here we give the name of the virtual machine.
$VMName = "HA_VM01"

# In the below set of cmdlets we create a virtual network adapter,
    virtual dvd drive, hardware profile and a disk
    drive for the virtual machine.
New-SCVirtualNetworkAdapter -JobGroup $JobGuid
    -PhysicalAddressType Dynamic -VLANEnabled $False
New-SCVirtualDVDDrive -JobGroup $JobGuid -Bus 1 -LUN 0
```

```
New-SCHardwareProfile -Owner "scvmm\admin" -Name "HWProfile"
  -CPUCount 1 -MemoryMB 512  -HighlyAvailable $True -NumLock
  $False -BootOrder "CD", "IdeHardDrive", "PxeBoot",
  "Floppy" -LimitCPUFunctionality
 $False -JobGroup $JobGuid
New-SCVirtualDiskDrive -IDE -Bus 0 -LUN 0
  -JobGroup $JobGuid -Size 40960 -Dynamic –Filename  "HAV_M01_
disk.vhd"


# Here we give the details of the virtual machine host on which
  this virtual machine will be created..
$VMHost = Get-SCVMHost | where {$_.Name -eq "Hyper-V01.admin.com"}
# Next we get the hardware profile and operating system
  which should be used for the virtual machine.

$HardwareProfile = Get-SCHardwareProfile | where {$_.Name -eq
"HWProfile"}
$OperatingSystem = Get-SCOperatingSystem | where
  {$_.Name -eq "64-bit edition of Windows Server 2008 R2
Datacenter"}

# next using the above set of input parameters we will
  create the virtual machine.
New-SCVirtualMachine -Name $VMName -Description "" -VMMServer
  "scVMMServer.scvmm.com" –Owner  "scvmm\admin" -VMHost
  $VMHost -Path "R:\" -HardwareProfile $HardwareProfile -JobGroup
  $JobGuid  -OperatingSystem $OperatingSystem -RunAsynchronously
  -StartAction NeverAutoTurnOnVM -StopAction SaveVM
```

- New-SCCloud: The New-SCCloud cmdlet allows you to create a private cloud in VMM. This cannot be done using the Hyper-V PowerShell cmdlets.

  The following sample code shows you how to create a private cloud using this cmdlet:

```
$Guid = [System.Guid]::NewGuid()
Set-SCCloud -JobGroup $Guid
$HostGroup = Get-SCVMHostGroup -Name "HostGroup02"
New-SCCloud -JobGroup $Guid -Name "Cloud02" -VMHostGroup
  $HostGroup -Description "This is a cloud for HostGroup02"
```

Summary

In this chapter, you learned the real integration scenario of using SCVMM to manage our Hyper-V infrastructure. In the next chapter, we will cover in detail how to troubleshoot Hyper-V environment issues using the best practice PowerShell cmdlets in Hyper-V.

6

Troubleshooting Hyper-V Environment Issues and Best Practices Using PowerShell

In this chapter, we will look at how to troubleshoot your Hyper-V environment using PowerShell. We will also look at how you can use **Best Practices Analyzer (BPA)** for Hyper-V to troubleshoot the environment. We have subdivided this chapter into two main sections covering the strategies that can be used to troubleshoot the Hyper-V environment:

- **Troubleshooting the Hyper-V environment using event log**: In this section, we will explore the built-in cmdlets in Windows that can be used to troubleshoot and analyze the Hyper-V events that get registered in the Windows event logs.

- **Troubleshooting the Hyper-V environment using BPA**: In this section, we will explore the Hyper-V BPA model-based cmdlets in the best practices module, which will be used to troubleshoot and verify whether the Hyper-V environment runs as per the best practice guidelines set by Microsoft.

Troubleshooting the Hyper-V environment using the event log

The Hyper-V administrator can use the Get-EventLog cmdlet to get the events related to Hyper-V. Monitoring these events using the **Event Viewer** GUI is a very tedious task. The following screenshot shows a view of the event log in the **Event Viewer** GUI. Scrolling through these events is a tedious task, as there are a lot of system-related events that are not related to Hyper-V:

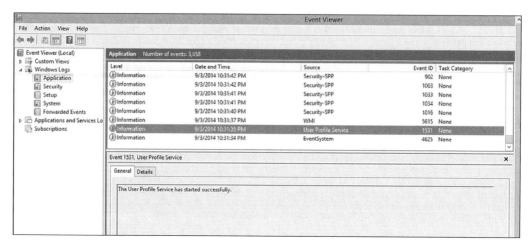

The Get-EventLog cmdlet can be directed to filter only the events that are related to Hyper-V. To do this, open up a PowerShell prompt in administrative mode and run the following command:

```
Get-EventLog system -source *Hyper-V* -after "07/21/2014"
```

The preceding command will query for all events related to Hyper-V in the system event log that occurred after July 27, 2014. Once we execute the preceding command, we will get the output returned as follows:

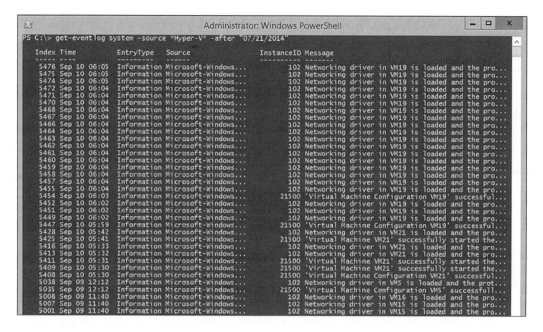

As you can see, I get all the required information filtered out from thousands of events that were registered in the event log. To make it simpler, the output from the preceding command can be used when executing the Out-GridView cmdlet to get a small GUI-based result. Type the following command in the PowerShell prompt to get the GUI-based result:

```
Get-EventLog system -source *Hyper-V* -after "07/21/2014" |
  Out-GridView
```

Just append the `Out-Gridview` cmdlet to the first cmdlet to get the result as shown in the next screenshot. As you can see in the following screenshot, I get a nice UI console for my results, which I can filter further by adding criteria:

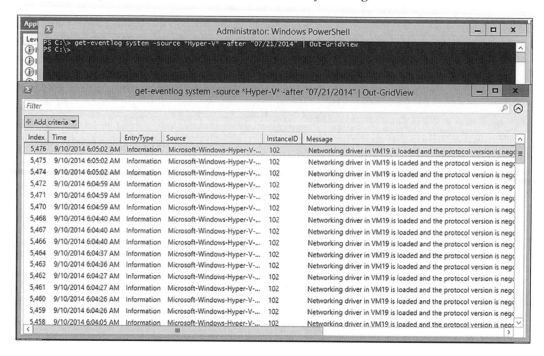

Hyper-V event logs can also be found at the application event log. These events have the `vmic` prefix on them. Run the following command in a PowerShell window and you will be able to see the Hyper-V-related event logs in the application event log:

```
Get-EventLog -LogName Application -Source vmic* -before "07/21/2014"
  | Out-GridView
```

The preceding command will query the application event log and get details of all the events for Hyper-V that happened before July 27, 2014 and contains `vmic` as the prefix in the source text. Another way would be to use the `Export-Csv` cmdlet instead to the `Out-GridView` cmdlet to save the output into a CSV file.

Troubleshooting the Hyper-V environment using BPA

The Hyper-V administrator can also use the BPA that is built in the Windows Server 2012 to test whether the Hyper-V environment is running as per the best practices guidelines set by Microsoft. Microsoft Hyper-V Best Practices Analyzer checks the current configuration set of Hyper-V against a list of recommended configurations and generates warnings and alerts when there are deviations. Microsoft Hyper-V Best Practices Analyzer will also provide solutions to correct the warnings.

There are a number of BPA models that are available from Microsoft. To select the right BPA model for Hyper-V; run the following cmdlet in a PowerShell prompt:

```
Get-BpaModel | Select Id
```

Once we execute the preceding command, we will get a list of all the BPA models that exist on the server, including the Hyper-V one:

```
PS C:\> Get-BpaModel | Select Id

Id
--
Microsoft/Windows/ADRMS
Microsoft/Windows/CertificateServices
Microsoft/Windows/ClusterAwareUpdating
Microsoft/Windows/DHCPServer
Microsoft/Windows/DirectoryServices
Microsoft/Windows/DNSServer
Microsoft/Windows/FileServices
Microsoft/Windows/Hyper-V
Microsoft/Windows/LightweightDirectoryServices
Microsoft/Windows/NPAS
Microsoft/Windows/RemoteAccessServer
Microsoft/Windows/TerminalServices
Microsoft/Windows/UpdateServices
Microsoft/Windows/VolumeActivation
Microsoft/Windows/WebServer
```

Once we get the correct BPA model for Hyper-V, we need to execute this BPA model against the server using the `Invoke-BpaModel` cmdlet. Execute the command shown in the following screenshot in a PowerShell prompt in administrative mode to invoke the Hyper-V BPA model against the server:

```
PS C:\> Invoke-BpaModel Microsoft/Windows/Hyper-V

ModelId           : Microsoft/Windows/Hyper-V
SubModelId        :
Success           : True
ScanTime          : 9/21/2014 11:19:32 AM
ScanTimeUtcOffset : -07:00:00
Detail            : {HYPERV01, HYPERV01}
```

Once the BPA model completes its execution against the server, we can get the results using the `Get-BpaResult` cmdlet:

Get-BpaResult Microsoft/Windows/Hyper-V | Group-Object severity

```
PS C:\> Get-BpaResult Microsoft/Windows/Hyper-V | Group-Object severity

Count Name                      Group
----- ----                      -----
   64 Information               {Microsoft.BestPractices.CoreInterface.Result, Microsoft.BestPractices.CoreInterface...
    4 Warning                   {Microsoft.BestPractices.CoreInterface.Result, Microsoft.BestPractices.CoreInterface...
    2 Error                     {Microsoft.BestPractices.CoreInterface.Result, Microsoft.BestPractices.CoreInterface...

PS C:\> _
```

As you can see in the preceding screenshot, we executed the `Get-BpaResult` cmdlet and grouped the output based on the severity and the result shows that we have 2 errors, 4 warnings, and 64 information messages.

Next, to filter out the BPA results to get only the errors in our Hyper-V environment, we need to execute the following command in the PowerShell prompt:

Get-BpaResult Microsoft/Windows/Hyper-V | ?{$_.severity -match
  "error"} | select modelid,source,category,title,problem,resolution

```
PS C:\> Get-BpaResult Microsoft/Windows/Hyper-V | ?{$_.severity -match "error"} | select modelid,source,category,title,p
roblem,resolution

ModelId    : Microsoft/Windows/Hyper-V
Source     : HYPERV01
Category   : Configuration
Title      : To participate in replication, servers in failover clusters must have a Hyper-V Replica Broker configured
Problem    : For failover clusters, Hyper-V Replica requires the use of a Hyper-V Replica Broker name instead of an
             individual server name.
Resolution : Use Failover Cluster Manager to configure the Hyper-V Replica Broker. In Hyper-V Manager, ensure that the
             replication configuration uses the Hyper-V Replica Broker name as the server name.

ModelId    : Microsoft/Windows/Hyper-V
Source     : HYPERV01
Category   : Configuration
Title      : Virtual machines should be backed up at least once every week
Problem    : One or more virtual machines have not been backed up in the past week.
Resolution : Schedule a backup of the virtual machines to run at least once a week. You can ignore this rule if this
             virtual machine is a replica and its primary virtual machine is being backed up, or if this is the
             primary virtual machine and its replica is being backed up.


PS C:\> _
```

The PowerShell community

PowerShell has great community support. The following section provides you with many useful links to the project page and forums:

- **Homepage**: http://msdn.microsoft.com/en-us/library/windows/desktop/

- **Manual and documentation**: http://technet.microsoft.com/library/

- **Wiki**: http://social.technet.microsoft.com/wiki/contents/

- **Blog**: http://blogs.msdn.com/b/powershell/

Summary

In this chapter, we covered how to troubleshoot Hyper-V environment issues using the best practice PowerShell cmdlets in Hyper-V. With the topics that we covered in this book, an administrator is expected to have a good understanding of using PowerShell to automate his or her administrative tasks for Hyper-V management.

Index

U

update management feature 96

V

virtual floppy drive (VFD) 37
virtual hard disks (VHD)
  managing, on virtual machines 39-44
  shared 9-12
virtual machine
  backups, managing with Hyper-V
    Replica 70-74
  configuring, to use ISO file 36
  configuring, to use virtual floppy
    drive (VFD) 37, 38
  connect, managing 75
  creating 29, 30
  creation utilizing ODX, reusable
    scripts used 78-82
  deleting 31
  exporting 65-67
  exports, managing 64
  export, updations 18
  generation 16, 17
  importing 65-67
  imports, managing 64
  live migration, reusable scripts creating
    for 83
  migration networks, managing 49, 50
  migrations, managing 63, 64
  network adapters, adding 53
  network adapters configuring, virtual
    switch used 51
  network adapters, removing 54
  network adapters, renaming 54
  network adapter VLANs, configuring 54
  network failover configuration 52, 53
  properties, configuring 33-35
  snapshots, managing 64-70
  starting 31, 32
  stopping 31, 32
  storage area network (SAN) 39
  VHDs, managing 39-44

virtual machine snapshots
  used, for managing exports 84, 85
  used, for managing imports 84, 85
virtual network adapters
  managing 48
virtual switches
  configuring 56-62
  creating 63
  managing 48
  removing 63
  used, for configuring virtual machine
    network adapters 51, 52

W

Windows Server Update Services
  (WSUS) 96

Thank you for buying
Microsoft Hyper-V PowerShell Automation

About Packt Publishing

Packt, pronounced 'packed', published its first book, *Mastering phpMyAdmin for Effective MySQL Management*, in April 2004, and subsequently continued to specialize in publishing highly focused books on specific technologies and solutions.

Our books and publications share the experiences of your fellow IT professionals in adapting and customizing today's systems, applications, and frameworks. Our solution-based books give you the knowledge and power to customize the software and technologies you're using to get the job done. Packt books are more specific and less general than the IT books you have seen in the past. Our unique business model allows us to bring you more focused information, giving you more of what you need to know, and less of what you don't.

Packt is a modern yet unique publishing company that focuses on producing quality, cutting-edge books for communities of developers, administrators, and newbies alike. For more information, please visit our website at www.packtpub.com.

About Packt Enterprise

In 2010, Packt launched two new brands, Packt Enterprise and Packt Open Source, in order to continue its focus on specialization. This book is part of the Packt Enterprise brand, home to books published on enterprise software – software created by major vendors, including (but not limited to) IBM, Microsoft, and Oracle, often for use in other corporations. Its titles will offer information relevant to a range of users of this software, including administrators, developers, architects, and end users.

Writing for Packt

We welcome all inquiries from people who are interested in authoring. Book proposals should be sent to author@packtpub.com. If your book idea is still at an early stage and you would like to discuss it first before writing a formal book proposal, then please contact us; one of our commissioning editors will get in touch with you.

We're not just looking for published authors; if you have strong technical skills but no writing experience, our experienced editors can help you develop a writing career, or simply get some additional reward for your expertise.

Hyper-V Network Virtualization Cookbook

ISBN: 978-1-78217-780-7   Paperback: 228 pages

Over 20 recipes to ease the creation of new virtual machines in the networking layer using Hyper-V Network Virtualization

1. Create, configure, and administer System Center 2012 R2 virtual networks with Hyper-V.

2. Design practical solutions to optimize your network solutions.

3. Learn how to control who can access a VM on a specific port to enhance the security of your virtual machine.

Windows Server 2012 Hyper-V Cookbook

ISBN: 978-1-84968-442-2   Paperback: 304 pages

Over 50 simple but incredibly effective recipes for mastering the administration of Windows Server Hyper-V

1. Take advantage of numerous Hyper-V best practices for administrators.

2. Get to grips with migrating virtual machines between servers and old Hyper-V versions, automating tasks with PowerShell, providing a high availability and disaster recovery environment, and much more.

3. A practical cookbook bursting with essential recipes.

Please check **www.PacktPub.com** for information on our titles

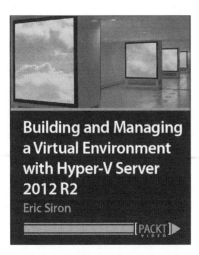

Building and Managing a Virtual Environment with Hyper-V Server 2012 R2 [Video]

ISBN: 978-1-78217-698-5   Duration: 03:30 hours

Build, deploy, and manage Hyper-V in failover cluster environments

1. Configure node computers for participation in a Hyper-V cluster.

2. Tackle the complicated subjects of storage and networking in a Hyper-V cluster.

3. Maximize the uptime for the services provided by your virtual machines.

Hyper-V Replica Essentials

ISBN: 978-1-78217-188-1   Paperback: 96 pages

Ensure business continuity and improve your disaster recovery policy using Hyper-V Replica

1. A practical step-by-step guide that goes beyond theory and focuses on getting hands-on.

2. Ensure business continuity and faster disaster recovery.

3. Learn how to deploy a failover cluster and encrypt communication traffic.

Please check **www.PacktPub.com** for information on our titles

Printed in Great Britain
by Amazon.co.uk, Ltd.,
Marston Gate.